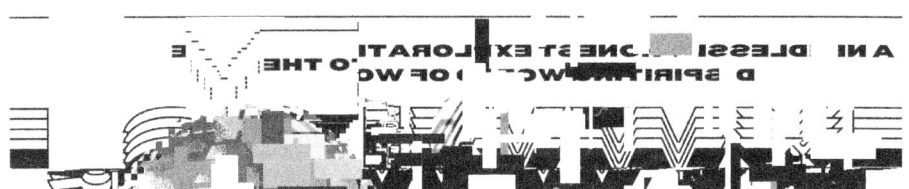

EVERYONE YOU WORK WITH IS A CUNT

A NEEDLESSY HONEST EXPLORATION INTO THE DISPIRITING WORLD OF WORK

AUTHOR'S NOTE

In a brilliant piece of timing, this book was being prepared, laid out and proof-read just as the whole world was knee-deep in a nasty virus. As a result it wasn't shared around for as much checking and proofing as planned - so all manner of basic grammatical errors and spelling disasters may well still abound.

If this offends and upsets you, I'd point out that you've either knowingly purchased or chosen to read a book called 'Everyone You Work With Is a Cunt' - so you've really given up any right to be considered someone with a reasonable opinion.

DEDICATIONS

I like my friends and family far too much to dedicate a book like this to any of them.

COPYRIGHT NOTICE

MISC

Iconography used in cover art and throughout was licensed via The Noun Project.

The font used for the titles is 'Bernoru' by Graham Paterson licensed via Creative Market

CONTENTS

REALLY?

You may read the title of this book and think, "That's just childish, sweary hyperbole and a ridiculously broad generalisation. Likely an attempt to justify a load of poorly constructed ranting and terrible jokes", but you'd be thinking wrong. Well, about the generalisation bit at least. I'll explain why.

In 2010, researchers from the Tyneside Institute of Strategic Economics were investigating the abnormal levels of staff turnover in certain industry sectors. In one strand of research[A] they plotted data from a number of studies, surveys and governmental statistical sources against their own well-regarded 'Byker Behaviour Perception Continuum'[B].

What they learned is that, in the general population, the vast majority of behaviour is perceived as reasonable or, at worst, indifferent. Only a small number of people are considered to be extremely positive or horribly negative.

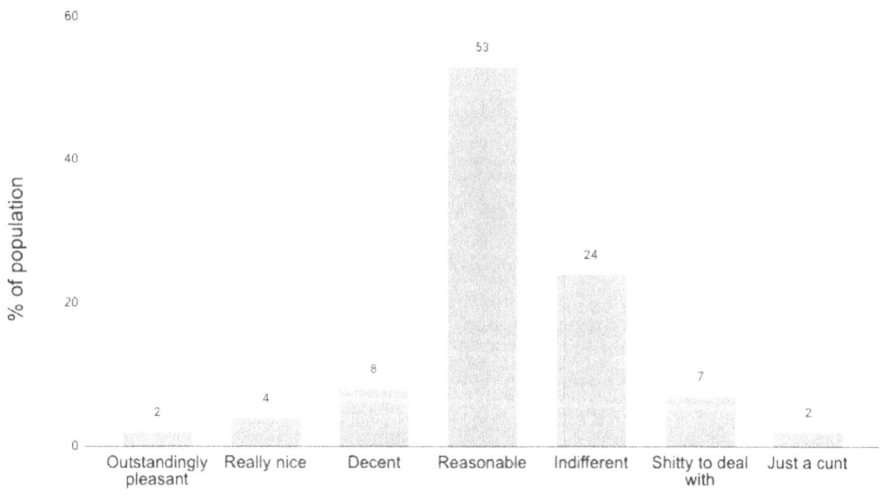

[A] 'Abnormal Staff Turnover in Motor Manufacturing', TISE, 2010
[B] 'Behaviour Perception In North Eastern Metropolitan Areas', Clegg & Harris, 2003

However, when the same analysis was applied to behaviour perceived during employment, a monumental shift down the continuum was revealed. Only a tiny amount of people were so outstandingly pleasant that the negative impact of going to work meant that their behaviour was perceived as reasonable - the results speak for themselves:

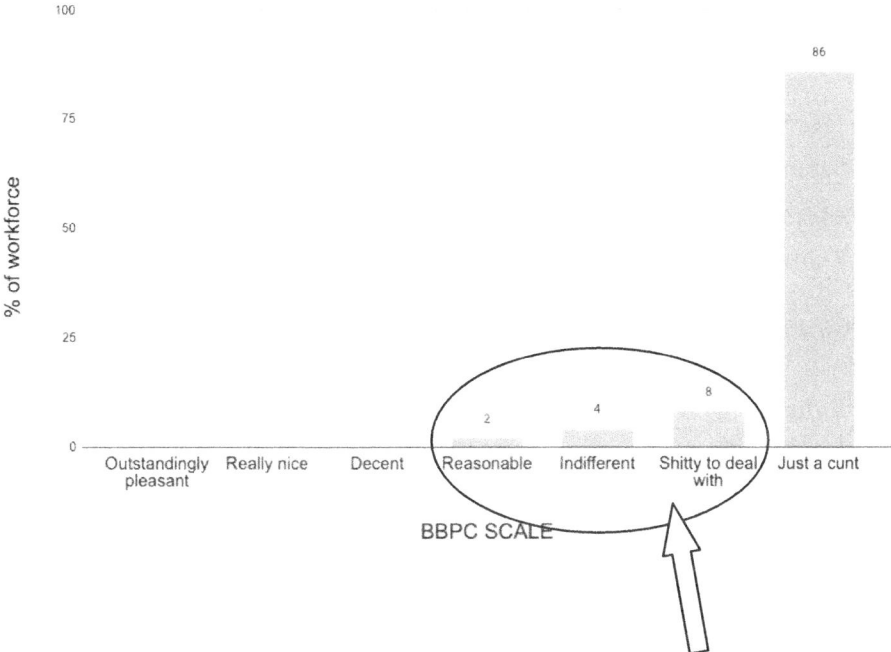

What the report didn't go on to say is that all the people ...here... are most likely to be employed in altruistic careers such as disaster relief work, charity volunteering, the medical profession, special needs teaching and caring for sick puppies. So you can be fairly sure which column the rest of us are in. Of, course there is the occasional glaring anomaly, the genuinely nice person that you work with - but think for a minute just how scarce and widely renowned such people tend to be.

So, yes, maybe the title of this book is a mild exaggeration, but '**Virtually All Of The People (Except For A Vanishingly Small Minority of Outstandingly Pleasant Individuals) That You Work With Are Cunts According To An Obscure Economic Study**' is just not a snappy title.

WHY? // 3P CONVERGENCE

Now that we have demonstrated that going to work turns people into complete monsters, we should probably at least have a cursory attempt at understanding why.

An example: *Your lovely neighbour, Sarah, who cat-sits for you while you are on holiday and does sponsored cake-baking for the local hospice, is known in the recruitment agency she works for as 'Ratfucker Sarah' - a nickname she coined herself after laying off half the staff and securing an obscene annual bonus in the process.*

The Sarah duality exists because of **The 3P Convergence Effect:**

Pounds (as in £): The term 'wage-slave' didn't appear from nowhere. Holding down a wage-paying job directly affects the quality of the rest of your life. This could be as drastic as affording to pay the rent, or as inconsequential as getting those carbon fibre cup holders added to your new Range Rover.

Moral fibre will crumble in the face of becoming skint, and ethical standards are no match for a pay rise. If you doubt this is the case, I refer you to how you feel looking at your bank balance during the week before pay day.

'Professionalism': Strictly speaking, being 'professional' means getting paid to do something. In the workplace, the term is more of a catch-all used to enforce a consensus of acceptable behaviour. If you are considered to be acting in an unprofessional manner, then you'll be in trouble asap. Things that are considered unprofessional include compassion, humour, forgiveness, personality, empathy and honesty.

Your job expects you to act like a sociopath, punishes you when you don't, and calls it 'being professional' as an excuse. If you think this seems a bit far fetched, I refer you to all of those amazingly disturbing psychological experiments from the 60s and 70s, where they proved that you can make people torture total strangers to death, as long as someone holds a clipboard nearby while they do it.

Power: Most jobs exist in organisations that are organised into a structure where a small number of people have power over (and responsibility for) what all the other people do. Frequently, individuals are put in charge despite no evidence of competence, expertise or leadership skills, instead being selected for displaying zealous 'professionalism', sucking up to (or sucking off) the management, or being part of the right social strata.

Power corrupts (and unearned power doubly so). It won't be long before Colin from the helpdesk will be acting like a tinpot dictator and shouting at people about their 'fucking timesheets', just because he brown-nosed his way into an assistant team leader role.

The flip side of this is that everyone else is, fairly consistently, resentful of the people that have undeserved, autocratic power over them. They will treat the people in charge with scorn and contempt at every possible opportunity.

Having a power-crazed, corrupt elite trying to control a resentful population using bureaucratic and economic means of enforcement is always going to end in tears. If you don't think this is true, I refer you to all of recorded human history.

When you consider that just one of the 3P factors can make a person act like an absolute tool, it is no surprise that the convergence of all three create a perfect (shit) storm...

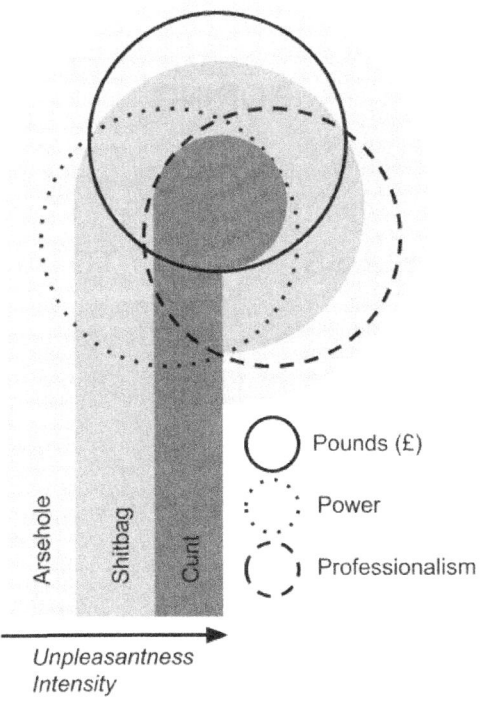

THERE ARE FIVE TYPES OF CUNT AT WORK...

The way that someone's awfulness at work will manifest itself is mostly related to what they do - as detailed in subsequent sections of this very book.

However, we can classify the workforce into five general types of cunt that transcend industry or role by plotting their level of income against their relative work life balance:

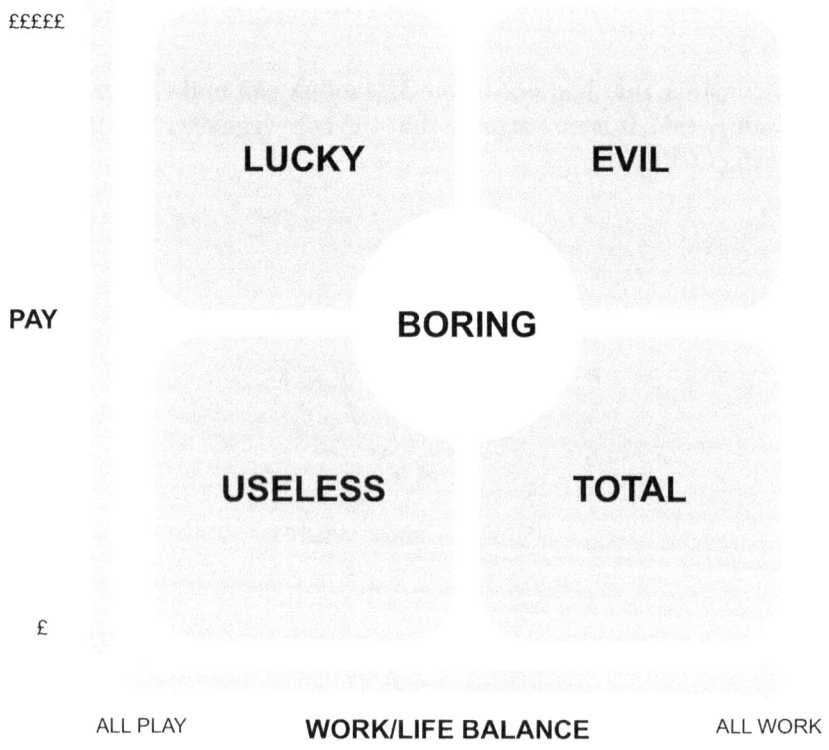

£££££

LUCKY   EVIL

PAY   BORING

USELESS   TOTAL

£

ALL PLAY   **WORK/LIFE BALANCE**   ALL WORK

...LUCKY

Complete bastards who seem to glide comfortably through life without having any discernible skill or talent.

The irritating product of good genes, rich parents, public school or nepotism, they live in an impenetrable bubble of confidence which protects them from the guilt and shame that make most people wake up screaming at night.

Examples include:

- Management consultants
- Gym instructors
- Anyone with the word 'Content' in their job title
- 'Mixologists'
- Professional DJs

Likely to say things like...

"The MD asked if can you finish that report for me, I've got to go to that ice cream tasting conference in Paris for the rest of the week."

"Please click like and subscribe to see more from my channel. All Patreon subscribers will get an Instagram shoutout from my gerbil, Kanye."

"Like Casper said in Cancun, YOLO bitches!"

9

...USELESS

Given even the most boring, repetitive and straight-forward tasks, these woeful specimens will find every single way to fuck it up. Maybe they mistakingly think they are too good to be pulling pints, maybe they are just too lazy to bother cleaning up after themselves, maybe they are just too stupid to understand the legal implications of sending dick pics via their work e-mail but they will always let you and themselves down.

Occasionally a useless cunt will transfer into the realm of lucky cunts via a scratchcard win. All useless cunts are habitual gamblers.

Examples include:

- Call centre employees
-'Baristas'
- 80% of people with the word 'Admin' in their job title
- Webmasters
- Local journalists

Likely to say things like...

"Have you got a reward card?"

"I can't come in today, I've lost my keys and I'm locked in my house"

"I'll have to speak to my supervisor, please hold." [The click of your call being cut off]

...TOTAL

People who are stuck in the annoying position of working a lot, but without the relative financial benefits. This category is associated mostly with those on some kind of 'career ladder'. They are either:

1) Auditioning to move up and become evil cunts - you will be a victim of their lust for power.

2) Trapped eternally in the career purgatory of pointless middle management - so they will have no qualms at all passing on all their misery and disappointment to you at every single opportunity.

Examples include:

- The other 20% with 'admin' in their job title
- Junior/middle management
- Police under the age of 35
- Retail managers

Likely to say things like...

"You didn't answer the phone within three rings earlier, so I've instructed HR to issue a written warning."

"Hi, my name is Kevin and I am really passionate about performance indicators."

"We need to talk about your lack of focus at the staff charity netball tournament last weekend"

...EVIL

These are the people that whining poets and conspiracy theorists generally refer to as 'the man'. They sit at the top of the pile because they like the sound of their own voices, think they are right about everything and have no problem with exploiting anyone and anything in the name of 'business', 'professionalism' or 'the national interest'.

The downside of this lofty position is that they have to work all of the time fuelled by paranoia, a barren personal life and the morbid need to accumulate as much money as possible before they die or get caught.

Examples include:

- Estate agents
- Barristers
- Hedge fund managers
- Tabloid journalists

Likely to say things like...

"I would love the chance to clear up the misunderstanding around the pension fund. Unfortunately, I cannot comment during legal proceedings."

"Would my right honourable friend, the Prime Minister agree..."

"It's not tax avoidance - It's wealth management."

...BORING

Dull, pedantic, uncooperative and soul-sucking - given enough time in one job or organisation, almost everyone ends up in this category.

The one time they will spring into action is if they get asked to do something that doesn't fit 100% into their job description. They will have an almost supernatural understanding of the demarcation between their job and any other. They will patrol this boundary and police any infringements with a zeal unmatched by even the most racist border guards.

Examples include:

- Chartered Accountants
- Management Accountants
- Auditors
- Anything to do with 'Procurement'

Likely to say things like...

"But the Mail on Sunday has such a good TV guide."

"I've written to my MP about the font change on the expenses form - why weren't we consulted on the switch to sans-serif?"

"So I complained that my starter only had four prawns instead of five and now I've got a 10% off voucher for the next time I stay at a Travel Lodge in Wales."

RETAIL

A LIFE SPENT WISHING THAT YOU HAD TRIED JUST A BIT HARDER AT SCHOOL

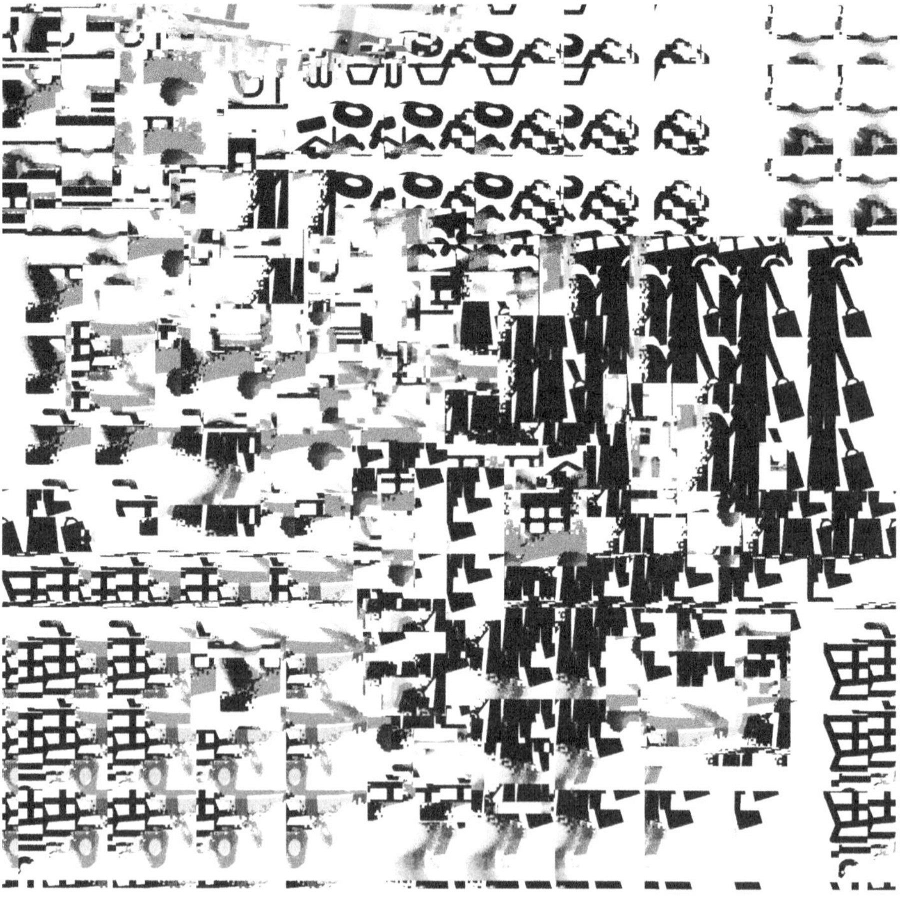

CLOTHES/FASHION STORES

People who work in clothes shops are like sponges. I don't mean that although they are classed as technically being alive they don't really do very much - although this is certainly true. A clothes shop employee absorbs the status and branding of their workplace to such an extent that they begin to believe that their social standing and self worth is directly related to the nature and reputation of the shop they work in. The more expensive and exclusive the shop, the more vile and unpleasant the people who work there - as illustrated by a couple of real-life case studies:

Charlie is 22 years old. Her main interests are YouTube nail tutorials, scratchcards and the absolute cheapest cocaine she can get her hands on. She dropped out of art college after 18 minutes, lives at home with her parents and is saving up for a cat. Charlie is an idiot, with all the depth of a birdbath and the mental agility of a houseplant. But, because Charlie left her job at Gap and now works in a hugely expensive section of a posh department store, she will treat you like a leper covered in dog sick if you dare to ask her if the price on that scarf is actually right. In fact you'll be lucky if she looks up from her phone at all.

Blake is a 25 year old tattoo addict who is waiting to re-take his GCSE English for the 9th time so he can land his dream job of trainee fitness instructor. His main hobby is sending pictures of (what he alleges is) his penis to women that annoy and confuse him, using the twitter account '@slut_handler6969'. Blake is a mouth-breathing, steroid-abusing moron with the vocabulary of a broken Speak and Spell and the charm of a used piece of toilet paper. However, because Blake is daft enough to work for below minimum wage, he has a job at a super trendy t-shirt shop. The shop is probably called something like 'K/RasH' - there are only 15 items on display, no sizes over medium and the prices are fully intended to trigger anxiety attacks. The lofty status conferred on him by this establishment means that Blake's idea of customer service is to behave as though he is the Lord of the Manor out leading the charge, while you are a grimy hunt saboteur that his trusty steed has just crushed underfoot. Unless you are a footballer, then he will act like a coy five year old.

CAR SALES

There is an unwritten rule in modern society that, on the whole, we don't blame people for unfortunate or abnormal actions that they are unable to control.

- You don't send forgetful little old ladies to prison for accidentally shoplifting a tin of baked beans. Little old ladies can't help it.

- You don't drop-kick a baby through a fence for shitting all over your lap. The baby didn't know you were wearing white jeans today.

- You don't burn down a car dealership and hunt down and torture all of the people who work there after they rip you off, ruin your credit rating and leave you ten grand in the hole with a car that so worthless that even the local fire service won't set light to it for practice. Car salespeople lie and cheat so much they don't actually know they are doing it.

The acceptance of scandalous dishonesty in the car retail world is so baked-in that going to shop for a car is a bit like being a willing audience member at an especially on-the-nose pantomime. We all play along with the teeth-sucking trade in valuation charade, we sit in subservient silence while they pretend to 'go and see the boss to see if we can do something on the metallic paint' and we smile warmly and die slowly inside at the transparent extortion of the range of credit agreements and schemes that they offer you like they are doing you a favour.

Part of the reason for our compliance is thinking about the alternative. If you don't buy a car from a dealer, then you are going to have to buy one from a private seller and unless you are a fan of trying to haggle with people with facial tattoos, or have always wondered exactly what is meant by 'receiving stolen goods', then this should be avoided like the plague.

A recent anthropological study into the dishonesty of car sales[X] revealed that the probability of dishonesty from an individual varies over the course of a career in the industry.

The study suggested that the degree to which someone is a lying fucking bastard is influenced and exaggerated by commonly shared workplace experiences. However, they were unable to disprove the alternative hypothesis that, if these people weren't such lying fucking bastards, then the commonly shared workplace experiences wouldn't have happened in the first place.

Unfortunately, the researchers were unable to extrapolate a clear nature vs nurture conclusion as to whether these thieving bastards are born or made - there is no reliable honesty data available on those who have yet to enter the industry. This is because no-one other than the criminally deranged grows up with the ambition to sell cars for a living.

The statistical evidence gathered was used to plot the percentage probability of a dishonest action or response against the age of an individual working in car sales. The results produced an unusual and abnormal distribution, which the research team dubbed The Bell(End) Curve...

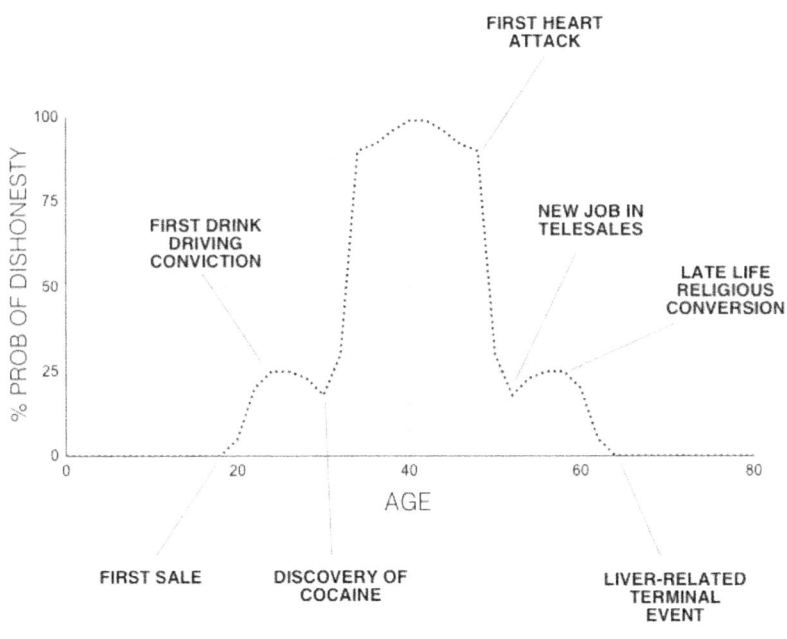

(X) "I Know Why The Caged Salesman Lies", Jones, Klepper & Smythe, 2013

SUPERMARKETS

No one is happy working at a supermarket. You wouldn't be happy either if you knew that you only have a job because computers can't reliably check if someone is 18 yet - and robots really can't deal with plastic bags.

There are four main categories of people employed in supermarkets:

1 - Student age dullards who were somehow too lazy, too dim or too scary to get a relatively cushy pub/restaurant job. They will tell you exactly what time they had to be in and how long until they get to go home, without you asking. Will throw your shopping at you with the velocity of an early 80's era West Indian fast bowler and continuous rate of an AK 47.

2 - People who fell out of the 'bad life decisions' tree and hit every single branch on the way down. Tired and sad looking, this lot are in it for the long haul, unless they can get on one of those long-term, high-risk drug trials that they keep applying for. Usually responsible for making those guttural and mangled announcements on the tannoy - the ideal showcase for their 30 a day habit. Their idea of a good day is getting put on trolley duty in the car park.

3 - Retired people who have had to go back to work. Will try to distract you from the fact that they don't know how a till works by being super friendly and chatty. Likely to comment effusively on absolutely every item you buy, until the strawberry lube arrives at their end of the conveyor belt and everything goes awkwardly quiet.

4 - Officious manager types who seem like they might be in charge of things. Being 'in charge of things' seems to mean flailing around the place wearing a flashing headset and shouting things like, "Take your break now!" or, "Can anyone cover Karen in cheese?" to absolutely no response. Their main job seems to be randomly closing checkout lines and leaving you waiting for the maximum possible amount of time before coming to approve your booze and paracetamol on the self-checkouts.

There is another layer of actual management who run things, but you won't be seeing them anywhere near a till, unpacking tins of beans or sorting out a 'clean-up on aisle 12' situation. They are too busy sitting in a darkened room somewhere trying to work out how to use new and exciting advances in technology to dehumanise their workforce even further.

CORNER SHOPS

Brighten up your next trip to the shop on the corner by playing a game of 'Mini-Supermarket Sweep':

1. Set a timer on your phone for 90 seconds.

2. Before the time runs out, locate and place as many different items on the counter that fit the following criteria:
> - Has fully intact packaging
> - Has an expiration date further then one month in the future.
> - Isn't clearly labelled, 'Not to be sold separately'.
> - Is not a knock off of a more famous brand using a vaguely similar logo and packaging.

How to score:

+10 points - each individual item on the counter that fits the criteria.

-15 points - any items on the counter that don't fit the criteria.

Bonus +25 pts - if you can get the person behind the counter to finish their phone call to serve you.

TECHNOLOGY SHOPS

A modern marvel of cohesive, vertically integrated, holistic customer fulfillment management.

It used to be that you would have to visit at least four different places if you wanted to:

- Experience aggressive sales techniques that even the motor industry would balk at.
- Be mis-sold a pointless warranty so worthless that its mere existence constitutes fraud.
- Get talked down to by a technical support expert who smells of cheese and piss.
- Have your holiday photos and personal data leaked to a wide audience.

Now you can do it in one tastefully designed, retail 'experience' location.

We are truly living in the future.

RECORD SHOPS

For the avoidance of doubt, we're not talking about the poor, useless bastards who have to work in the big chain entertainment stores (never has the badge proclaiming 'I'm happy to help' been less true), we're more concerned with the 'specialist' end of the market here.

Dense, intimidating and complex - and that's just the smell - any specialist record shop is a strange and confusing place. They manage to break normal economic models by managing to separate you from as much money as possible, while deliberately making you about as welcome as sand in a condom.

Everyone who works in a record shop regardless of age, gender or race is called Steve (or at least a word that sounds a bit like Steve) - it's really more of a title than a name at this point. More judgemental than your septuagenarian, Daily Mail-reading, magistrate neighbour. More pretentious than a morse code poetry recital. More condescending than a P.E. teacher in a room full of asthmatics. Having to deal with a Steve is hard work, encountering a group of them is a truly gruelling experience (incidentally the correct collective term is an 'adjudication' of Steves).

Record shops are of course, the home of Record Store Day, an annual example of late capitalism so grim that academics use it to create theoretical models of post-apocalyptic societal collapse. This being the case, we'll leave it to one side and instead consider two of the main day-to-day scenarios that can play out in a record shop:

Scenario A: You are shopping for a particular record

Good luck finding anything you might actually be looking for. The records are arranged into categories that you're sure they have made up for a laugh, then ordered according to the star sign of the artist's paternal grandmother.

After spending longer than you would have liked searching through 'Trash Wave', 'Grind Lounge' and 'Homeostasis' - you realise that you are going to have to go and ask. Deep down you know that this is going to be bad.

Despite glaring at you while you were nervously scouring through 'Vanilla Analogue', Steve will now be doing something else, forcing you to raise your voice above the level of the obscure Dub Jazz that they will refuse to turn down. Having yelled your request for some late 90's indie album across the counter - brace yourself for the response.

Steve will pull a face like you have just asked them to fellate an elephant, before letting out a huge sigh and letting you know that they "don't really tend to sell that sort of thing". The word 'thing', will be intoned in the way that most people reserve for discussion of only the very, very worst Balkan war crimes. As you begin to turn away, dejected and deflated, Steve will mutter "Do you want me to order it in for you?" with such withering contempt that you are somehow compelled to agree. Steve will then tap away at a very old computer keyboard, trying very hard to hide the fact that they are buying the record off Ebay and multiplying the price by three in their head.

You leave £50 lighter, empty handed and bewildered at what has just happened.

Scenario B: General browsing leads to a random purchase

While flipping through the 'Slow Gazebo' section you find a re-issue of an old album by a favourite band, one you don't have. It costs roughly five times as much as the CD alternative because the record is made of purple vinyl. Fuck it! You've just been paid and something like this is probably an investment isn't it?

The likely response of the Steve at the counter as you present your purchase will be almost indistinguishable from someone who has just had a warm bowl of dog diarrhea placed in front of them.

If somehow you have chosen to purchase something so insanely obscure that even a Steve can't be unimpressed, then they will say something like: "Yeah... not their best though, really". At this point it is crucially important that you do not engage in any sort of discussion or argument. In the best case you will end up leaving with another three painfully expensive and unlistenable records. In the worst case you will end up changing your name to Steve and working in a record shop.

THE OFFICE

WHERE COMPASSION, HOPE AND PERSONALITY GO TO DIE

HR

Theoretically, this is the part of your organisation that is supposed to deal with all the difficult 'soft' issues around staff behaviour and well-being. The fact that they chose to call it 'Human Resources', like something that George Orwell threw out of the first draft of 1984 for being too oppressive and harsh, really does give the game away.

East Germany had the Stasi, Russia has the KGB, the place you work has a HR Department.

HR are collaborators, they are traitors, they are the spineless sci-fi movie characters who say, "Well, I for one welcome our new Intergalactic overlords", and then help to hunt down the human resistance in exchange for being spared from the alien food factory.

Like all of the most effective evil, life in the HR department may seem deceptively banal. A closed shop of eternally pregnant women and pale young men in knitted tank tops sit around gossiping about all of the most sensitive details in the personnel files. "Ooh, you'll never guess who had a non-descended testicle!" they cackle, while feasting on the baked goods, made for them by staff from other departments paying terrified tribute, like ancient Greeks chaining a local virgin to the sacrificial rock for the Kraken.

Sometimes this all gets a bit much and they have to take a break and relax by spending hours talking about soap operas and RuPaul's Drag Race while drinking hot chocolate out of stupidly oversized mugs. There is no one working in HR in the UK who is not a member of Weight-Watchers.

When you actually need something from them, then the scary, bureaucratic, formal stuff kicks in very quickly. If you dare to do something as outrageous as change your address, or enquire as to why you haven't been paid for three months, then brace yourself for a torrent of official meetings and endless form filling.

If you ever get in proper trouble at work, someone from HR will inevitably sit in on the bollocking. Their purpose in the meeting is to look stern and superior, while taking detailed notes so that they can report back to their colleagues exactly who it was that you told to "fuck right off, you total nonce". They will recommend disciplinary action based on the quality and frequency of any cake-based offerings you have made.

PROJECT MANAGEMENT

Choosing a career in project management is a bit like carrying around a big sign with "I HAVE NO DISCERNIBLE REASON FOR BEING ALIVE" written on it.

NOTE: The sign in question will be spelt wrong, fall apart after half an hour and took three weeks longer that the original estimate of ten minutes to deliver.

Never, ever pay any attention to anything that a project manager says. They don't know what they are talking about. Don't be deceived if they wave a diagram at you or some sortof plan. It is all a charade to try and make it seem like they serve some purpose, which they don't.

They will use stunningly boring terms like 'Baselining', 'Exception reporting', 'Business Case' and 'Gantt Chart' – all designed to make you think they are doing something. The truth is that you can replace a project manager with a pack of post-it notes and a biro. The only perceptible difference is that things will get done quicker.

Tasks	Month 1	Month 2	Month 3	Month 4	Month 5	Month 6
Procrastination						
Aimless Meetings						
Random Delegation						
Excuse Generation						
Shameless Blameshifting						

PROGRAMME MANAGEMENT

Project management but on higher wages, pretty much exactly the same except that to replace them you will need a family pack of post-it notes and two or three biros of different colours.

24

BUSINESS ANALYSTS

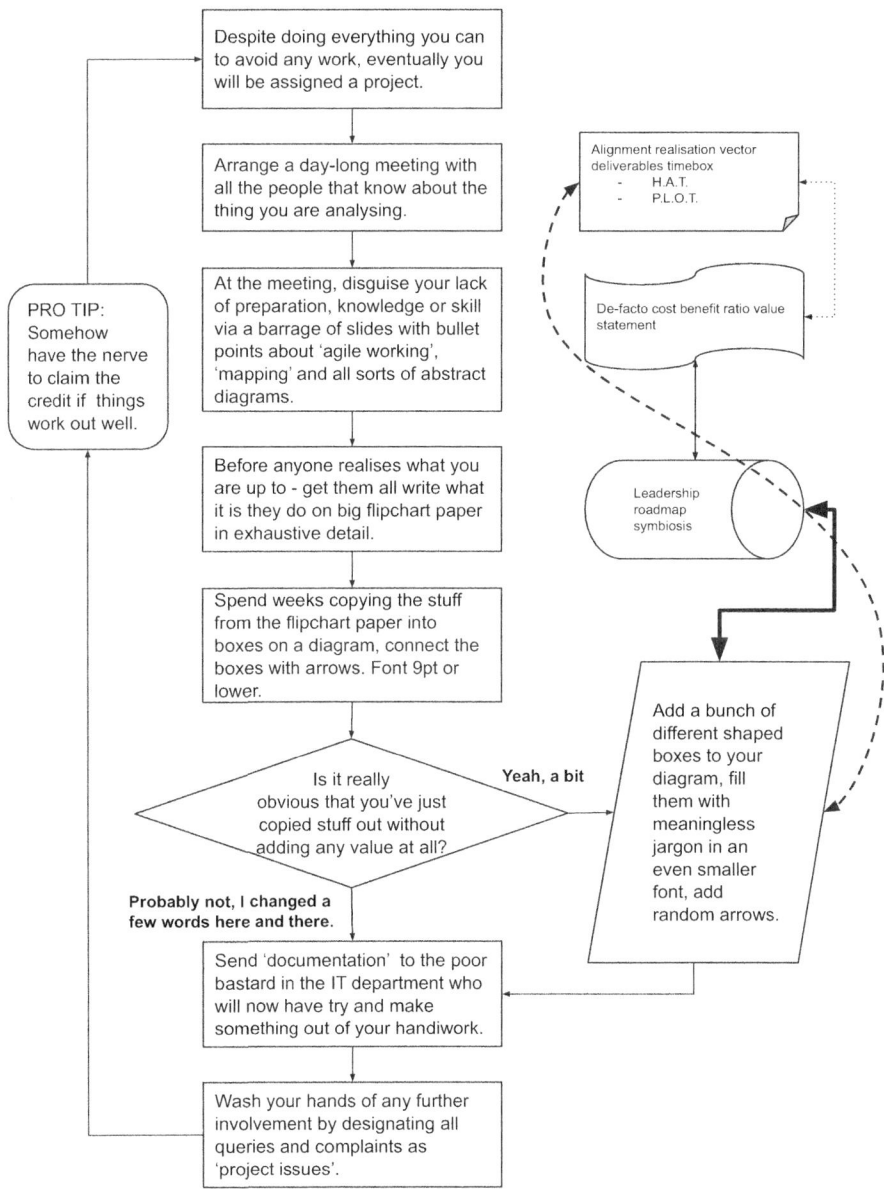

Despite doing everything you can to avoid any work, eventually you will be assigned a project.

Arrange a day-long meeting with all the people that know about the thing you are analysing.

Alignment realisation vector deliverables timebox
- H.A.T.
- P.L.O.T.

At the meeting, disguise your lack of preparation, knowledge or skill via a barrage of slides with bullet points about 'agile working', 'mapping' and all sorts of abstract diagrams.

De-facto cost benefit ratio value statement

PRO TIP:
Somehow have the nerve to claim the credit if things work out well.

Before anyone realises what you are up to - get them all write what it is they do on big flipchart paper in exhaustive detail.

Leadership roadmap symbiosis

Spend weeks copying the stuff from the flipchart paper into boxes on a diagram, connect the boxes with arrows. Font 9pt or lower.

Is it really obvious that you've just copied stuff out without adding any value at all?

Yeah, a bit

Add a bunch of different shaped boxes to your diagram, fill them with meaningless jargon in an even smaller font, add random arrows.

Probably not, I changed a few words here and there.

Send 'documentation' to the poor bastard in the IT department who will now have try and make something out of your handiwork.

Wash your hands of any further involvement by designating all queries and complaints as 'project issues'.

THE COMMS DEPARTMENT

A refuge for people who are so poor at journalism that they can't even hold down a job writing stories about slightly perturbed pensioners and escaped pets for the local advertising rag. This, however, doesn't stop them all thinking that they are some kind of latter-day Hemmingway - but with a devastating flair for puns and a deep appreciation of how often to use exclamation marks (!!).

Despite what they think, no-one outside your company gives a flying fuck whatever it is that goes on in there all day. So bereft of any chance of dealing with actual newspapers or journalists these feckless souls will spend a large amount of their time creating internal news stories, usually for some kind of staff newsletter. The style and content of these literary efforts have the medicated blandness you would normally associate with propaganda from the most rudimentary yet brutal totalitarian regimes.

For Example:

Adrian Goes Nuts and Makes A Big Splash!

There was plenty of 'interest' in the finance office last month when junior accounts payable clerk, Adrian Ogilvy, completed a sponsored swim in aid of a local squirrel sanctuary. Adrian (27) completed a magnificent thirteen and a half lengths of the nearby municipal pool, a feat that was described as "a reasonable effort" by duty lifeguard and swimming expert, Ray Potshaw (43).

Speaking to us afterwards Adrian revealed, "It was tough going but I just kept thinking about the squirrels and I was able to battle through the pain. I've never done more than nine lengths before and I'm totally puffed out! I'm so tired I may need to hibernate!"

Mrs Cheryl Weathership (54), proprietor of Grey Tails Squirrel Reserve was delighted to receive a cheque for £29.62 that will "go towards some twine and possibly some nuts". She was also quick to pay tribute to her aquatic benefactor, "I can safely say that I have never met anyone quite like Adrian," she gushed, "Sometimes he just stands there watching the squirrels for hours, even in the rain." Her furry friends must certainly think that Adrian is tree-mendous!

PERSONAL ASSISTANTS

First off, we need a bit of historical context here:

The idea to rename the role of 'Secretary' as 'Personal Assistant' was an evil genius piece of management bullshit. By making those in the role feel more important, it was possible to expand their responsibilities and workload, giving them more to do, while crucially, not paying them any more money.

Unfortunately the cynical management consultants who came up with this rebranding were too busy high fiving each other and awarding themselves another line of blow to consider any potential downsides. Due to the huge and largely unwarranted boost to the newly minted PA's ego, they now believed that they were actually superior to everyone - apart from the person that they personally assisted. This was despite the fact that they were still, in essence, a glorified typist who answered the phone in a put-on posh voice and checked a diary now and again.

Cut back to the current day - and the ego of the average PA is now so bloated and outsized that they genuinely seem to believe that they play an integral part in keeping the place that they work running successfully. This would certainly be true if business success and profitability were dependant on factors such as:
- Not even nearly understanding how a computer, photo-copier or printer works.
- Going out for a fag every fifteen minutes.
- Having the highest possible percentage of desk and wall space being covered in pictures of children.
- Acting like being in charge of the cupboard where the post-it notes and whiteboard markers are kept is a solemn duty, equivalent to guarding the nation's nuclear deterrent.

Most PAs are living vicariously through the lives of their teenage daughters. You will have to listen straight-faced while they boast endlessly about how young Kym is going to do a BTEC in Broadcast Journalism and is currently going out with a slightly older, professional man. In actuality, her little princess is widely known for the subscription-only streaming videos she makes round the back of the nearest Nando's, sometimes accompanied by her drug-dealing beau and the local college admissions tutor.

27

SALES

Imagine being trapped inside an episode of 'The Apprentice' that never, ever ends.

For many people, the prospect would be enough to trigger immediate suicide. Worryingly, there is a small, but significant segment of the population that see this as an ideal work environment.

Sales is the place where your financial compensation is directly related to the size of your ego, the depth of your dishonesty and the intensity of your desire to fuck over absolutely anyone so that you can get those limited edition alloys on your Mercedes.

It doesn't matter if you are selling complex financial derivatives, half finished IT systems or novelty sex toys based on the movie 'Avatar'. To be successful in sales you need to be a hyper aggressive bullshitter with the social conscience of the Ebola virus and the compassion of a date rapist.

You must be sociopathic enough to believe that the ends justify the means, even when the ends are 'enough commission to get a second hot tub' and the means are 'ripping off people with learning disabilities by selling them bogus, but somehow legal, bitcoin investment schemes'.

The Alec Baldwin 'Always Be Closing' scene in Glengarry Glen Ross has a lot to answer for.

ACCOUNTING & FINANCE

Accountancy, contrary to its popular image, is the career home to a wide and varied group of people. From those who may have only fantasised about torturing and killing a lone backpacker through to those with fully planned (and costed) campaigns of serial murder, there is room for each and every kind of repressed homicidal psychopath in the world of accountancy.

It is little wonder that they are all sitting there waiting to go completely postal when you consider that what they do is so utterly, soul-destroyingly dull, abstract and pointless.

Someone in accounts will actually have one of those battered 20 year-old signs on their desk that will say: "You don't have to be MAD to work here, BUT IT HELPS!!!". Never, ever go within ten feet of this person, if you do they will kill you, fuck your corpse and eventually eat your remains. You have been warned.

SECURITY

Generally the domain of people who have been thrown out of the army, or are just too fucking weird to get into the police, but would still like to wear some kind of quasi-military uniform everyday.

In any organisation you are likely to have two encounters with the security department. The first will be when you start and they take the most unflattering picture possible for your ID badge. The other contact will come in the form of a spectacularly illiterate e-mail telling you that:

a) Someone has broken into the building and stolen some company property or some poor bastard's wallet.

b) It is the fault of staff for not being a bunch of uber-suspicious vigilantes who shoot on sight anyone a bit shifty looking.

A reasonable person might well ask where these guardian angels were during such a crime wave. The answer is that they were in their 'Security Bunker' carrying out "pro-active security and surveillance practices". In other words they were sat in a pornography-adorned room somewhere in the basement – smoking, sleeping and knocking one out over CCTV footage of the managing director's personal assistant.

LINE MANAGEMENT

Like diabetes, there are two types of line management, both of which can cause pain, disorientation and require medication to alleviate symptoms.

Type 1: These are the reluctant, wage-slave line managers, forced into a supervisory role in order to keep their job and pay the rent, or frequently as a result of becoming a parent and needing more dosh. So they not only have to deal with a load of screaming, dribbling and shit-based situations ('Shituations'), they then have to go home and deal with a baby too.

Type 1s usually have an actual job to do as well, so will generally leave you well alone until you fuck something up so comprehensively that someone further up the chain of command notices. The flip side of this laissez-faire approach is that if you ever actually need them to sign or approve something, you'll need the investigative skills of Hercule Poirot to track them down to the coffee shop, spare bedroom or park bench where they are hiding from the madness.

Type 2: This where line management is brought on by elective and deliberate actions. A type 2 line manager is a complete nightmare for every member of their team as well, as all of their team's family and friends. Everyone's going to be hearing an awful lot about "that fucking jumped up little twat, Darren".

Having no career goals, other than to be able to boss people around, a type 2 manager has hardly any practical skills, so don't expect any help, advice or support with your work. What you can expect is a slavish and pedantic approach to company rules, office policies and staff directives - the more minor and pointless the better. They are never happier than when blind-copying half the HR Department in on an 'written warning' that they have been forced to issue to you after you were thirty seconds late for the second time in eighteen months.

Always make sure that you are nowhere near a type 2 line manager when the phrases 'appropriate office attire', 'suspended on full pay' or 'disciplinary investigation' are used - they will noisily and spontaneously orgasm.

MIDDLE MANAGEMENT

The unwritten motto of corporate middle management is 'All Surface - No Feeling'.

You may think that competence, expertise and leadership are the three qualities most likely to elevate someone up to the well-heeled corridors of middle management. In actuality the three criteria that are most vital are:

- Looking important.
- Sounding important.
- A job title that is both important sounding and impenetrably vague, to the point where it sounds like it might be a joke.

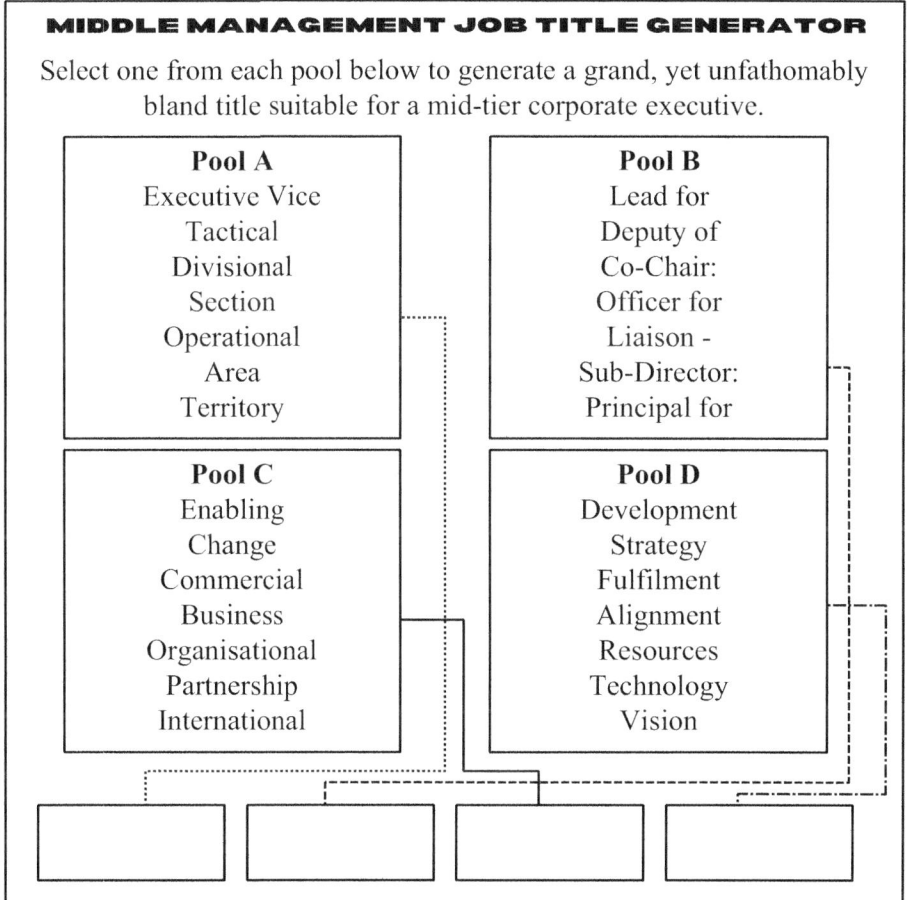

MIDDLE MANAGEMENT JOB TITLE GENERATOR

Select one from each pool below to generate a grand, yet unfathomably bland title suitable for a mid-tier corporate executive.

Pool A	Pool B
Executive Vice	Lead for
Tactical	Deputy of
Divisional	Co-Chair:
Section	Officer for
Operational	Liaison -
Area	Sub-Director:
Territory	Principal for

Pool C	Pool D
Enabling	Development
Change	Strategy
Commercial	Fulfilment
Business	Alignment
Organisational	Resources
Partnership	Technology
International	Vision

SENIOR MANAGEMENT

These are the wrong ways to determine whether someone is important enough to be considered 'senior management':

- Hundreds, maybe even thousands of people work for them.
- They earn an obscene amount of money.
- They have a big penthouse office.
- They travel by helicopter.

This is the correct way to establish that someone should be classified as 'senior management':

When they completely fuck things up, the net effect of any consequences is positive.

This may seem counterintuitive - and for everyone else it certainly isn't the case. If the average employee was covertly filmed in the office, wearing a pair of novelty antlers and masturbating frantically to moose porn, then they'd be out of a job immediately and probably unemployable for years. But if the moose enthusiast was a captain of industry and the leaked footage led to a share price tumble followed by mass lay offs and suicides, the person in question would be quietly paid off, spend a couple of months at some exclusive facility and then re-emerge on the board of some other multinational (as well as a new highly paid non-exec position with some wildlife preservation charity).

This 'failing upwards' effect was statistically modelled by the Latvian Institute of Econometrics[L] in the years following the last financial crash. It was an attempt to understand why authorities around the world chose not to send the people who ruined the whole world to prison, instead punishing them by giving them a shit-tonne of free money.

Their research, summarised in the Complete Fuck Up Curve, (reproduced opposite) showed that the financial impact of completely fucking up reduces gradually as the impact of the fuck up in question increases.

No-one has been able to precisely quantify the exact variables and characteristics needed by an individual to move into net-benefit territory, with one obvious exception: Government, where you can catastrophically fuck up and experience potentially exponential benefits. If you can fuck things up more completely than anyone else, you'll get a country to run.

THE COMPLETE FUCK UP CURVE

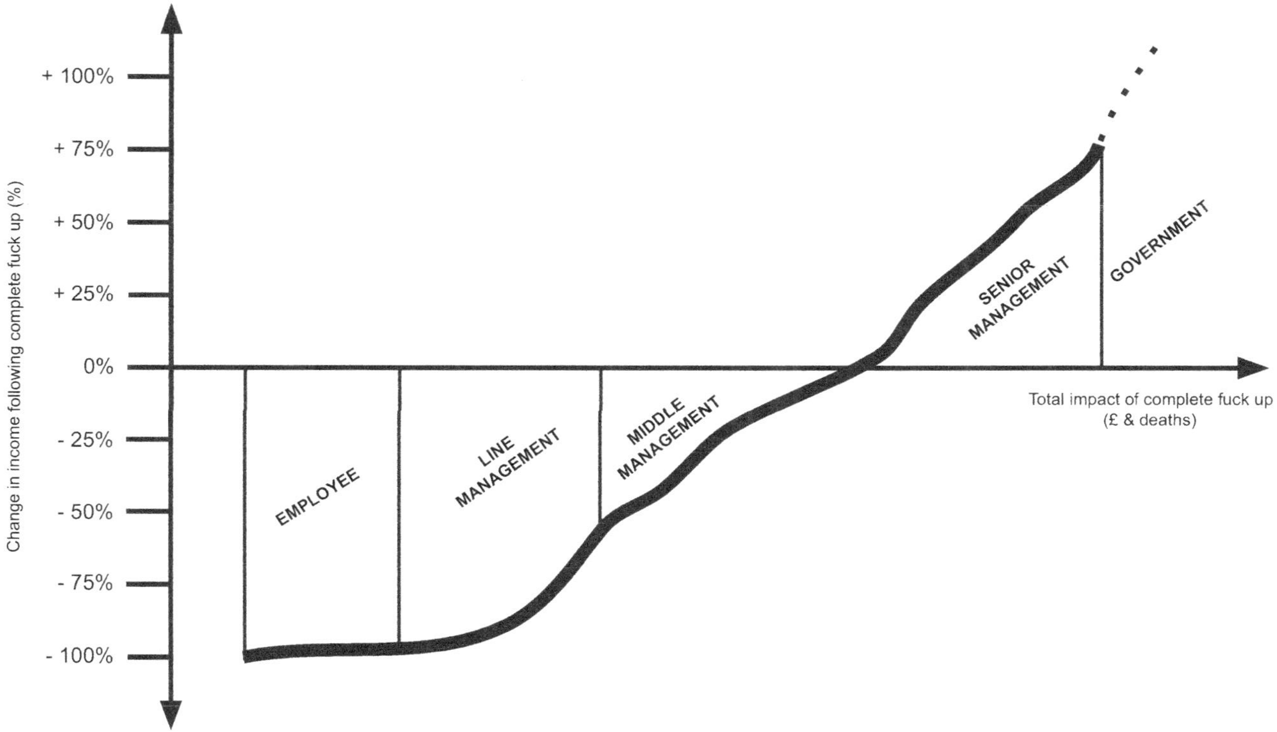

Change in income following complete fuck up (%)

- 100%
- 75%
- 50%
- 25%
0%
+ 25%
+ 50%
+ 75%
+ 100%

EMPLOYEE

LINE MANAGEMENT

MIDDLE MANAGEMENT

SENIOR MANAGEMENT

GOVERNMENT

Total impact of complete fuck up
(£ & deaths)

(L) "Why Aren't These Bastards Behind Bars?", L.I.E, 2011

33

TEMPS & CONTRACTORS

There are many different types of people who choose to work on a temporary or contract basis. Some say they enjoy the flexibility, others cite the need to fill a gap between seasonal work, while a worryingly high number need to make ends meet while perfecting their edgy comedy juggling act.

Whatever pretence they are hiding behind, there are really only three reasons for having a temporary contract rather than an actual job:

1) Having no useful skills, talents or knowledge.
2) No one trusts you at all.
3) Tax dodging.

Examples that you may well have come across include:

The 'Wet-Dream Imbecile'

An incredibly attractive specimen somewhere in their early twenties. The magnitude of their trouser-tenting or gusset-dampening desirability will only be matched by their absolute inability to do anything remotely useful.

Destined to alienate everyone of the same sex immediately and get all their work done for them by the other side. After managing to set off the fire alarm while opening a packet of biscuits, they will leave to go travelling with some other ridiculously gorgeous but spirit-crushingly vacuous idiot.

The 'Post-Graduate Dullard'

Has a first-class degree in post-modern Peruvian cinema, so has doomed themselves to a life of menial office work. Likely to look a bit like Mr Bean and exude all the charisma of a traffic bollard. Will never, ever leave even if you stop paying them.

The 'Total Fucking Liar'

The CV looked too good to be true and it turns out that it was. Congratulations, you have got a total fucking liar on the payroll for as long as it takes to get rid of them. It should only be a couple of weeks, so get them to make you endless cups of coffee to keep you awake while you end up doing all the work that they were supposed to be capable of.

The 'Australian That You Want To Kill'

Apparently Australia is the best fuckin' place in the entire fuckin' world. The sports are better, the beer is better, the girls are better, the weather is better and so on. All of which begs the question: Why leave this sun-kissed, non-stop party utopia to come and be a poorly paid data-entry clerk in a faceless corporate basement in London? Is it really just so you can take the piss about the cricket?

The 'Genuine Mystery'

No-one remembers when they started, no-one knows who hired them and no-one has any clue as to what they are supposed to be doing or even what their name is. One day they won't be there any more, no-one will mention it.

The 'I'm Too Good For This'

They got third in Business Studies from a university so marginal that you haven't even heard of the county that it is in. They are still living at home with their parents, or more likely have been "so totally kicked out" with a fifty grand down payment on the sort of flat that you will never, ever afford.

Almost entirely useless, they will be put in charge of things like ordering office furniture. Will fail to win any friends by banging on loudly about how they are going to be a DJ or a fashion designer and how everyone that works here is such a loser and how they haven't even got decent cars – eventually they will fuck off and get a job as a management trainee at Poundland.

The 'Consultant'

Swings into your organisation in a cloud of expensive scent and bewildering confidence. Management will swoon at their feet and throw stacks of cash at them, while everyone else will wonder how on earth they get away with:

- Making everything they come into contact with at least 50% worse and 100% more expensive.
- Hiring in all their mates onto equally lucrative contracts to be paid for via staff lay offs.
- Spending half their time lining up their next contract, probably at the company they've just persuaded your Board to spend a shitload of moeny with.

Six months after they leave, another consultant will turn up to try and deal with all the problems the last cohort left in their wake. Guess how that goes?

CALL CENTRE

If you are lucky enough to work somewhere that has a call centre (essentially a large air-conditioned Victorian workhouse) then you will have run into these people, probably in the corridor, maybe on the steps outside the office, certainly in the canteen, hanging around vending machines in the smoking room and lurking near the bookies across the road – basically anywhere but in the call centre answering the fucking phone.

The irony is that whenever you see one of them, steadfastly avoiding whatever it actually is that they get paid for doing, they are on a mobile phone moaning about how awful their job is.

Generally not the healthiest looking bunch in the world, in fact, call centre operators tend to look a bit like extras from Dawn of the Dead. Don't be fooled though, they are in fact blessed with th physical flexibility of a yoga master and the visual acuity of a hawk - physical attributes honed into perfection by hours of playing iPhone games under their desk using toe-based gestures.

To be fair, if your entire working life was governed by a flashing board and a contract that stipulated to the nearest second how long you are allowed to take to have a shit, you'd probably skive off too.

FACILITIES MANAGEMENT

Lazy, sweaty men in bad suits whose responsibility extends to hiring caretakers, looking after some sets of keys and forgetting to get your twatting radiator fixed.

Tend to labour under the misapprehension that because they have some kind of minor property surveying diploma, from some no-hoper college in Fuckstead, Arsehampton, that they are in fact a major architectural talent.

If you phone up to report a stiff window handle don't be surprised if they get all Richard Rogers and tell you that what you really need is some kind of baroque balcony bolting on to the side of your office.

IT SUPPORT

There is an old cliché that IT departments are full of gawky, twenty-something males with the social skills and personal hygiene of a dead dog.

These days, nothing could be further from the truth; many of the gawky, socially inept males in the IT world are now well into their forties and only smell as bad as a terminally ill dog (albeit on a very hot day).

Of course their nervous anxiety goes out of the window if you dare to question them on a technical matter. Such as how come your fucking computer still doesn't work after they have spent two days in your office, supposedly fixing it, but actually trying to take photos up some girl's skirt. At such a time, they will address you with the sort of condescension you might expect from Steven Hawking if he were explaining quantum physics to Paris Hilton and then eventually re-install your PC, making sure you lose all your work to teach you some sort of lesson.

These strange men are the tip of the IT iceberg. Hidden from public view, the IT department will also provide a sanctuary to a hive of computer programmers: Strange troll-like creatures of indeterminate age, they feed off striplights and are allergic to any form of non-digital communication.

If you ever get an e-mail from a programmer it will almost certainly have some sort of Star Trek/Wars/Lord Of The Rings reference in it with absolutely no trace of irony.

HOSPITALITY

THERE IS A REASON THAT 'HOSPITALITY' CONTAINS THE WORD 'HOSPITAL'

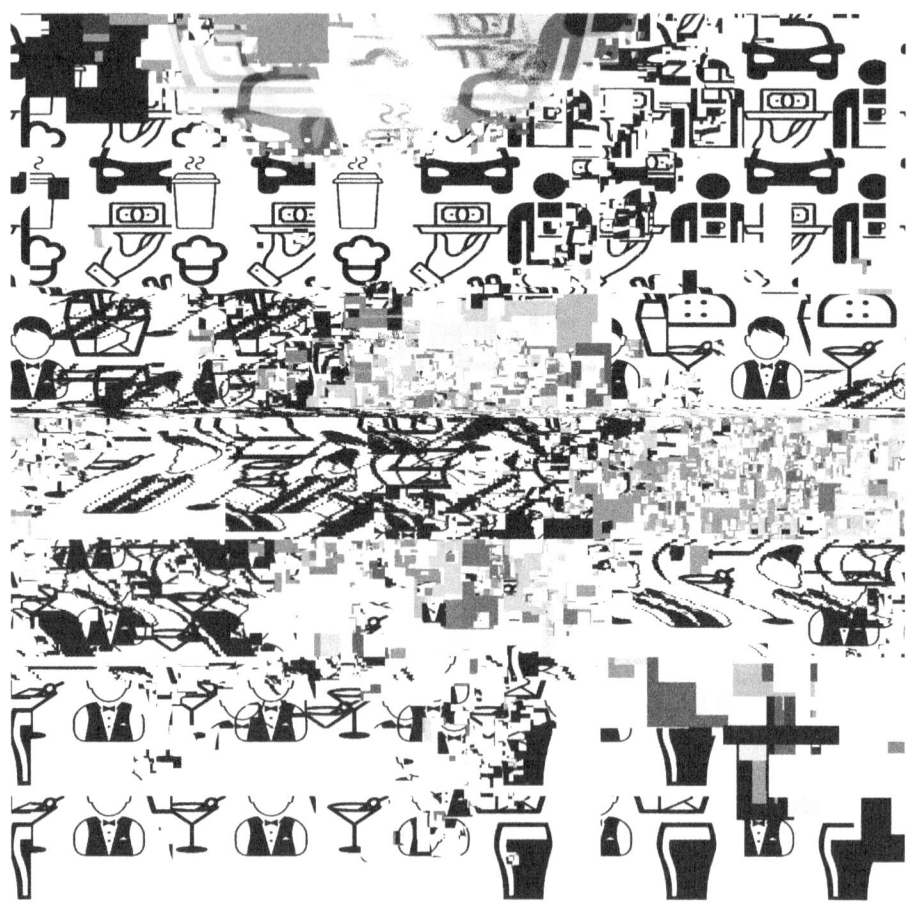

CHEFS

Did you always want to be a shouty man in the army, but were afraid to take your clothes off in front of the big boys? Do the words 'relentless workplace bullying' cause a warm feeling in your sex parts? Can you turn on an oven?

Chances are you're already a chef.

There are many different types of chef, with many interesting prefixes such as 'Sous', 'Executive' and 'Commis'. Despite whatever continental wankery they add to their job title, you can be sure that substance abuse problems and personality disorders are the, ahem, order of the day.

Whether dabbing speed into their gums to get through another shift at some trading estate carvery, or sticking crack up their bum before making an ironic foie gras Pot Noodle dish somewhere in Shoreditch - all chefs are on masses of drugs. This is because working in a kitchen is supposedly super stressful and tiring. Of course, the reason that working in a kitchen is so stressful and tiring is because the people running the place are on loads of drugs. It is a vicious circle that would be funny if the future of your gastro-intestinal health wasn't in the mix.

You may feel sorry for the people working under these culinary dictators, what with all the bullying, yelling, appalling working practices and barely legal pay practices. The bitter truth is that they are all waiting for the day when they can afford just enough crystal meth to behave just as appallingly as the despot that currently rules the roost. All for the glory of making people shouting "Yes, Chef!" when asked if the prawns for table four are out of the microwave yet.

WAITING STAFF

The following is reproduced (without permission) from 'UK Hospitality
Staff Accreditation Scheme - Waiting Staff: Intermediate'.

UKHSAS - W/S Intermediate - REF R443/09P
8 of 14

Tick one box	Question 7. How should you greet new arrivals?
	A - Warm but respectful greetings - show them to their table, offer to take coats.
	B - Grunt, "Table for how many?", then point to where they should go. Wander over briefly to wordlessly wipe the table with a damp cloth.
	C - Let them hover awkwardly by the door for long enough to feel really uncomfortable. If they have a reservation, tell them that their table is being prepared and let them wait a bit longer. If they don't have a reservation, suck your teeth, sigh and make a big show of looking through your reservations despite the fact that your establishment is clearly 95% empty.

Tick one box	Question 8. A customer is getting angry because his food hasn't arrived yet, what do you do?
	A - Immediately prioritise the production of said meal with the kitchen, offer profuse apologies and a complimentary drink.
	B - Ask, "What did you order?", in the manner of a barrister cross examining a witness. Traipse into the kitchen to find out that you forgot to write it down properly. Head back to the customer and inform them "the chef is just doing it now", despite knowing full well that it will be bloody ages.
	C - Duck into the kitchen, locate the missing meal. Stick a finger as far as you can up your arse and then rub it across the top of their steak.

Tick one box	Question 9. A customer wants to send their food back and wants a replacement meal, what is the ideal course of action?
	A - Remove the meal immediately, ascertain the issue with the customer and ensure that the problem is rectified to their satisfaction - remove the cost of that meal from the bill.
	B - Take the meal back to the kitchen, rearrange slightly, bung in the microwave for two minutes and return to the customer.
	C - Inform all staff that a 'Code Green' is in progress - a two minute warning to get as much saliva, mucus and phlegm into the offending meal as possible. Provide the replacement meal to the customer, almost keeping a straight face while telling them that the kitchen sends their 'apologies'.

40

Tick one box	Question 10. How should you check that a table is enjoying their meal?
	A - At the most opportune moment, once everyone has their food, make a quick enquiry and efficiently deal with any issues.
	B - Exactly three seconds after the first person on a table starts eating, suddenly appear and enquire, "Everything alright with your meals? Yes? Great", and then vanish as rapidly as you arrived.
	C - Once the main course is concluded, ask if everything was ok when you are taking the plates away. If anyone gets particularly moany, make a mental note, so that a 'Code Yellow' can be implemented if any desserts are ordered.

Tick one box	Question 11. What is the best way to ensure you get a healthy tip from a table?
	A - Provide a polite, unobtrusive and efficient service throughout the dining experience.
	B - Wait ages to supply the bill, grunt, "Service isn't included", as you slap down the paperwork with a couple of six year old boiled sweets.
	C - A relentless campaign of artless and creepy, innuendo-based flirting with the most attractive person on the table.

TAXI DRIVERS

No one wants to talk to you in the pub, the newspaper never prints the e-mails you send them every week and you've been banned from Twitter, Facebook and, somehow, the UKIP message board. But if drunk people want to get home from the pub on a Friday night they'll have to listen to you then won't they?

Once you've picked them up it's best to start with something low key and relatively inoffensive - maybe distract them with some jovial bigotry about that Polish bouncer while you make sure that the meter is in 'double time' mode, or even better, not working at all.

Once you are underway and have established that no-one is in any state to risk an argument with you, then you can shift gear into some lofty political discourse. Why not kick off with your thoughts on immigration reform?

If anyone takes offence you can always offer them the alternative of getting out of your fucking cab. You pay your taxes and you've got a right to free speech - that's what that stuck-up prick at the soft play centre didn't understand.

By now you should be free to hold court on any an all subject you like, perhaps segue into some of your thoughts on why there isn't an International White Men's Day while you stick on a bit of Stereophonics or some other proper fucking music.

Is that girl in the back laughing at you? Does she want to bloody walk? Well, does she? No, I didn't think so. She should have some fucking respect - didn't she see your Help For Heroes sticker?

Are you going to be sick mate? Do me a favour - hold it in for five minutes. while I tell you about how the British Empire civilised the world.

DON'T TUT AT ME LOVE. THATS A FUCKING HISTORICAL FACT. LOOK IT UP. THEY'VE GOT THE RIGHT IDEA IN THAILAND IF YOU ASK ME. BRING BACK HANGING. BREXIT MEANS BBRRRREEEXXXXXXXIIIITTTTTTT.

Right, that'll be forty-seven quid mate. No mate, cash only. No, I don't have any change.

Have a good night.

THE SIX STAGES OF TAXI JOURNEY RACISM

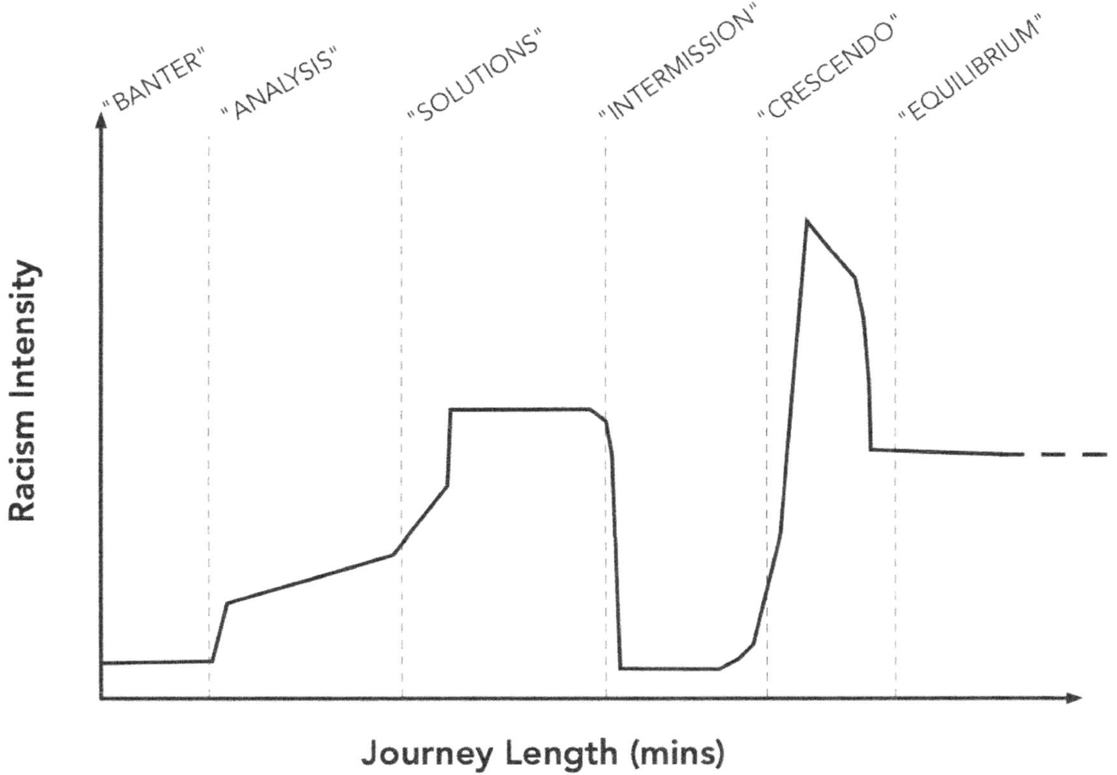

Racism Intensity

Journey Length (mins)

"BANTER"

"ANALYSIS"

"SOLUTIONS"

"INTERMISSION"

"CRESCENDO"

"EQUILIBRIUM"

BARISTAS

Looking back across the lifetime of the Earth, there are a number of huge watershed moments that once crossed could never ever be reversed. Changes of such significance that the fate of the planet was permanently altered.

When the creatures now classified as Acanthostega first began slithering from the ocean onto the land, life on earth was set on a course that would fundamentally change the face of the world, leading inexorably to the evolution of human beings.

At the moment that the atomic bomb was dropped on Hiroshima, geopolitics changed forever and introduced an ever-present existential threat for every person on earth.

In a similar way, at some distinct and yet vague point in the more recent past we decided as a society to adopt the idea of 'person that makes cups of coffee' into an actual career with its own stupid name. The full, long-term impact on the world of work, the macro economy and maybe even the future of civilisation has yet to be realised. But I think we all know that it won't be good.

Somehow, as a species, we have tricked ourselves into thinking that pouring hot water into a cup, making banging noises and stamping small pieces of cardboard is an artisanal endeavour, comparable to painting a fresco or penning an epic poem.

In years to come we'll look back and realise that this is when the collapse began, the downward spiral towards the dusty, post-apocalyptic wasteland was all the inevitable consequence of some bloke called Darren getting ideas above his station because someone was overly impressed by the way he sprinkled cocoa powder on a milky coffee.

TAKEAWAY PROPRIETORS

Some people are born great liars, some become great liars, others have the need to be great liars thrust upon them - if you run a takeaway the chances are it is all three.

Making a success of any kind of takeaway business relies on having absolutely no scruples at all, plus the ability to defend complete bullshit with such a straight face that you should really be negotiating peace in the Middle East rather than flogging stray cat Chow Mein to the lazy and inebriated.

The lies are relatively small to begin with. That order won't really be ready in 20 minutes and you know it. The picture of the Value Burger Meal on the illuminated sign is not even slightly reminiscent of what the customer will end up receiving. The thick, hefty looking burger in the picture surrounded by a fresh looking salad garnish and plump sesame bun will actually resemble a disc of cardboard, soaked in Bisto, compressed between two big scabs and delivered in a dirty styrofoam mouse coffin.

Everyone expects these lies of any takeaway, but where these nasty bastards take it to the next level is the moral ease with which they forge hygiene certificates, tipp-ex over use-by dates, bribe health and safety officials and proclaim tasty dishes of "succulent lamb in a tantalising spicy sauce" while knowing full well that they are dismembering abandoned dogs out the back.

Also, while you are waiting for your pigeon and chips to finish in the microwave, they only ever have yesterday's Daily Express for you to read.

Bastards.

PUB LANDLORDS

In 2003, a thought experiment named 'The Landlords Conundrum'[Y] was widely circulated in academic circles. It was notable at the time as an example of using philosophical methods to answer two very practical, if enigmatic questions:

1 - Why the fuck would anyone want to run a pub?
2 - Why do most pub landlords have an approach to ethics that would make the devil himself stand and applaud?

ASSUMPTIONS:
- You are a (mostly) functional alcoholic misanthrope, aged between 30 and 50.
- Your body has seen better days. You don't like getting up in the morning.
- You are obsessive about touching young women in a less than appropriate manner.
- Young women absolutely do not want you touching them.
- You are unable to understand the concept of sell-by dates on snacks.

Given these assumptions, do you either:

a) Resign yourself to a life spent mostly in prison?
b) Cut a long story short and commit semi-accidental suicide while enjoying internet pornography with a freezer bag over your head?

So, while it is easy to be appalled by a landlord syphoning Aldi whisky into Glenlivet bottles, or registering their VAT account in their dog's name, we must consider that they are acting out of financial desperation, eager to stay in the one career likely to keep them away from the inside of a cell, or the end of a noose fashioned from plastic bags.

What is horribly astounding is the general acceptance of the industrial level of sexual harassment that landlords seem to get away with. It is only a short, but horribly well-trodden path from, "The Guinness isn't going to change itself", to "The toilets aren't going to unblock themselves", before a brief stop at, "Your rent isn't going to pay itself." Before arriving at the eventual, inevitable destination, "It's not going to suck itself." Everyone in a relationship with someone that runs a pub probably used to work for them. Yuk.

[Y] 'One For The Road', Lassky & Holmes, 2003

TYPES OF BAR STAFF

The Professional

Somehow, over the course of too many years, too many opportunities squandered, too many failed relationships and too many broken promises, working behind a bar has ended up as their career. They might be putting a brave face on things, but you can tell they aren't happy about it. Never without either a cold sore or a black eye.

The Criminal

A cash-in-hand maniac who has worked in every local boozer, moving on when their drug dealing or till-diving reaches a level where the boss is able to overcome their very real and entirely reasonable fear and give them the boot (via text message, whilst on holiday, ideally in another time zone). Very likely to have a teardrop tattoo, or one of those neck spiderwebs.

The Tortured Artist

There they stand, resplendent in their 'Godspeed! You Black Emperor' t-shirt, gazing in horror and disbelief at the pub full of drunk revellers singing along to the cover band doing another encore of 'I'm A Believer'. You can tell they would prefer to be literally anywhere else, but bar work is the only thing that will fit in with their 'day job' of songwriting for 'Proficient in Excel', the post-lounge art-rock band that they play bass in. Never, ever ask them about the screenplay that they are working on.

The Student

A young person genuinely offended by the outrageous abuses of patriarchal capitalist oppression - such as having to get to work on time. The really annoying ones will sit reading a notoriously heavyweight book in between serving customers. When you appear at the bar and they have to put down 'Being and Nothingness', prepare yourself for a glare that could melt steel.

The Eye Candy

Reality TV rejects who just need to earn a few quid while getting their instagram followers into four figures. Outrageously flirty, but with the short term memory of a brain injured goldfish - never attempt to order more than two drinks at a time from one of these. Will be a nexus of gossip, drama and sexual harassment claims, but can get you a discounted gym membership.

47

PUBLIC SECTOR

LIKE A REAL JOB, BUT WITH

THE CRUSTS CUT OFF

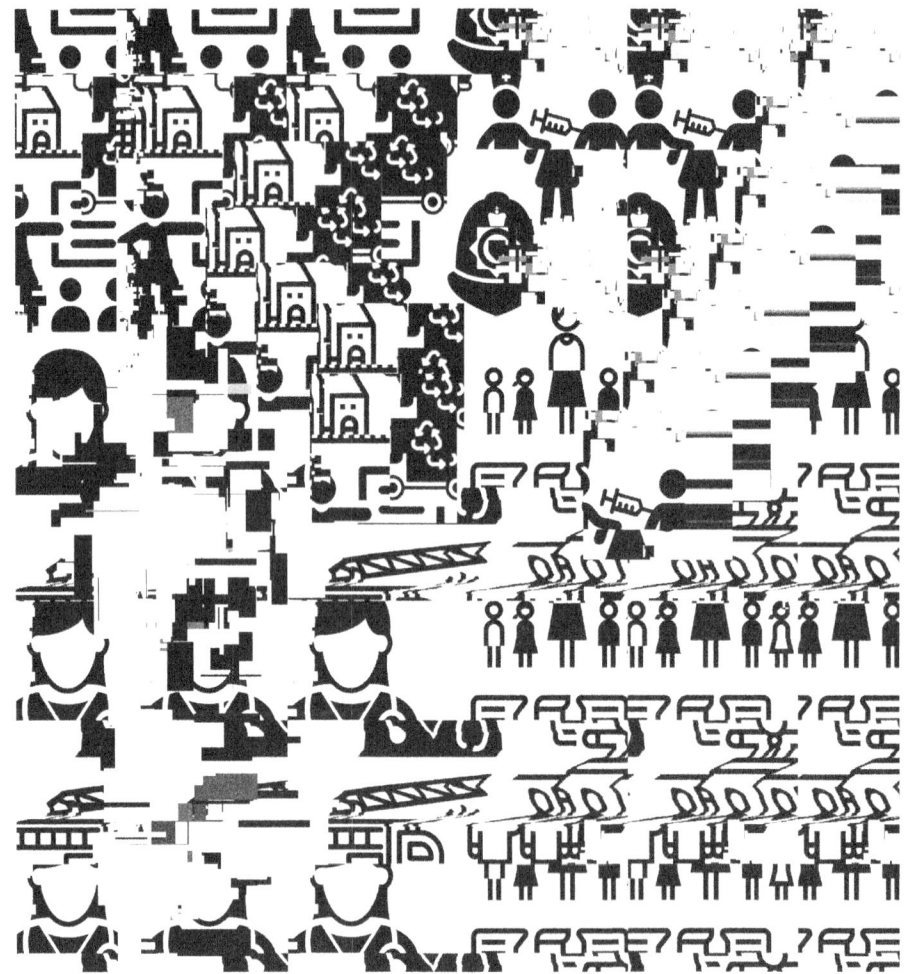

BINMEN

Despite appearances, 'Binmen' is not actually a gendered word, but instead a generic term of ancient and long forgotten antecedence.

According to scholars of ancient Mesopotamia, a word '*Been Mah-an*' appeared in many ancient scrolls and documents[T].

The literal translation of Been Mah-an is '*second oldest profession*', which doesn't immediately make much sense. However, when you consider just how popular the oldest profession was in ancient Mesopotamia, the need for someone to regularly take the resulting mess away becomes more apparent.

The modern incarnation of the Binman is an unusual and often troubling individual. Despite looking about as healthy as a retired footballer's liver, most binmen seem have the strength and endurance of the average ultra marathon runner.

You shouldn't be able to run about the place, hoisting heavy bins two at a time while chain-smoking evil roll-ups. But they do - and I think we should all let it remain a mystery as to exactly how.

The exception to the whole desperately ill/explosively athletic vibe are the geezers who drive the trucks, who just look desperately ill. They pin up pornography and take back-handers for disposing of evidence, while chasing the dream of one day maybe driving far enough in one go to get into third gear.

[T] 'Refuse & The Ancient World', British Museum, 1978

TEACHERS

A note on nursery/primary school teachers: This section will focus purely on secondary school teachers. Primary school teachers are obviously weird, but if most of your time was spent in rooms where the furniture was half its normal size you'd probably go a bit mad too. Clearly anyone who voluntarily spends their time in the snotty, shitty world of small children so that the rest of us don't have to is taking one for the team and, as such, has suffered enough.

Imagine for one terrible moment you are fourteen years old and back at school. Back at some grim, prefabricated, soul-sucking, arsehole factory. Ambition, joy and creativity being gradually beaten out of you, both figuratively and literally. Picture the uninformed, uniformed masses milling through the corridors and sitting bored senseless in every classroom. Breathe deep and drink in the atmosphere - and by atmosphere I mean smell - a heady mix of cleaning fluids, wet clothes, stale cooking aromas and every flavour of Lynx deodorant.

Now try to imagine yourself as the sort of person that, stuck in this hellhole, thought to themselves, "I want to spend the rest of my life in a place like this". Chilling.

It is easy to trot out the old cliche that 'those that can, do - those that can't, teach' - but just because something is easy, it doesn't mean you shouldn't do it. Cliches are generally only cliches because they are true.

There are many ways we could choose to categorise teachers: body odour, primary personality defect, hair grease and degree of eye-redness are all good options, but to really examine the subtle differences involved we should probably go subject by subject:

English: If you had to try and teach Shakespeare to feral children who communicate mostly through grunts and emoticons you'd be depressed too. Always sucking mints between lessons to hide the aroma of vodka, sipped from the hip flask that they are desperately trying to make last until at least 2pm. Live in constant fear of not knowing what previously benign words have been adopted as teenage slang for 'good', 'bad' and 'anal sex'.

Maths: They might know what a quadratic equation is, they might be able to teach you how to calculate the internal angles of a hexagon, they might even be able to explain the Fibonacci sequence. They don't seem to know how to brush their fucking teeth though. Most dentist's nightmares are about maths teachers.

Languages: The smuggest of all teachers and the third most likely to have sex with their students (or more likely the chain-smoking French ones they get exchanged with). Happy to perpetuate the dangerous idea that you will be able to survive and thrive in any foreign locale as long as you are able to find the nearest post office and swimming pool.

Science: The teaching equivalent of Spiderman - a geeky exterior with a highly developed sixth sense for imminent danger and destruction. Rather than the result of a radioactive spider bite, this skill has developed as the result of spending most of their time in a room full of children playing around with fire, electricity and hazardous chemicals. Also like Spiderman, they probably still live in their aunt's spare room.

IT: If you can't get an actual job working in IT, then there must be something very, very wrong. Probably best if we leave it there.

Geography: This gang of rock botherers live for the days when they can get out of the classroom and act like a middle aged, paunchy Bear Grylls on some kind of field trip to an especially rainy part of Wales or Scotland. Their students are also happiest during these fresh air excursions, because Geography teachers usually have the kind of body odour that can discolour brickwork and trigger nosebleeds.

History: Demonstrate their devotion to the study of past events by proudly displaying the evidence of at least their last six meals on their crusty, unwashed clothes. The type of teacher you are most likely to see knocking back sad lunchtime pints should you ever find yourself back in the vicinity after you've left school.

PE: The alphas of the teaching pack, these cold shower enthusiasts are easily distinguishable by their 'ran through sports direct while covered in glue' clothing style and ostentatious collection of keys. Never happier than when they get to join in sports with children half their size. Never sadder than when they have to cover another subject, which they do by making you read a textbook in silence while they gaze out of the window at the rugby posts like a widow waiting for a soldier who is never coming home.

Art: There are two types of art teacher: the first are joss-stick scented acid casualties, who just want you to express yourself and enjoy inhaling solvent fumes. They put all the weirdest art work on the walls, making their classroom look like a serial killer's jail cell. Secondly, there are the failed professional artists who sit and do their own work in the corner leaving you to sketch something they pulled out of skip that morning. They delight in evaluating each drawing in turn, in front of the whole class, with the withering contempt usually only seen by judges on TV talent shows.

Craft/Design etc: Practical masochists who have found a job that lets them indulge in their passion for minor self harm on an almost hourly basis. Will pay virtually no attention to your woeful attempts to make a spice rack, or stab each other with chisels, as they quietly plan the most plausible accident that will allow them to drill through the tip of their thumb.

Drama: The teaching equivalent of those terrifying mothers who tart-up their prepubescent daughters for bizarre beauty pageants. Will treat your school's bare-bones production of Romeo and Juliet as an exercise in Kubrick-ian perfection, with a direction style based on throwing tantrums at twelve year old kids and diving out for sneaky cigarettes. The second most likely type of teacher to have sex with one of their students.

Music: Probably had an early dalliance with the entertainment business that ended unhappily - now they deal with their own performance anxiety issues through the ritualised musical humiliation of adolescent children. Those that still write and perform music are the teachers most likely to have sex with their students. There is no more sad and pathetic court exhibit than the track listing of a self-made EP (probably named something like 'Love Detention') found by a suspicious parent...

POLITICIANS

A successful politician will have a thick skin, loads of confidence and the stubbornness to ignore any error and plough on regardless of actual competence. These are the perfect characteristics for a street performer, but maybe not so great for someone whose job description may involve public safety, economic policy and a nuclear arsenal.

Some time ago, politics was described as 'showbusiness for ugly people'. The remote and corrupt halls of power were mostly populated by crusty old geezers, who looked like semi-decomposed bank managers and were drawn from the fields of law, trade unions and the aristocracy.

These days, it's 'ugly business for show people' as politics becomes ever murkier and our leaders are increasingly drawn from a shallow pool of semi-celebrities, PR scumbags, failed journalists and the aristocracy.

Standards were never exactly high to begin with but now they appear to have fallen off a fucking cliff, and with the ongoing parade of political shitstorms the world is experiencing it seems likely that there is some way to go before we eventually hit the rocks.

To grasp the total shittyness of the modern politician and to better understand the mess we are in, perhaps it is best to consider the reasons any individual decides to enter politics:

1) Wanting to change the world for the better - and having the huge, ridiculous ego to think that you are just the person to do it.

2) To shamelessly make as much money as possible by squeezing every possible perk and advantage out of your position. Every action you take will be for the benefit of whoever is willing to pay you the most for it.

3) Because you are the willing tool of an ancient, sinister society. Following a ritual that involved you masturbating into a recently sacrificed animal, the dark lord himself appeared and bestowed upon you the task of attaining supreme political power in order to further his diabolical schemes. Also, expenses.

4) The sex. The weird, borderline-legal, transgressive, unpleasant, inexplicable sex.

5) Because the more important you become, the harder it will be for your

past crimes to catch up with you.

6) *"Just fell into it really. After my gap decade, Daddy wanted me to go and work at his fund in the city - but finance is just such a bore and I'd have to be in the office by nine every day! I didn't spaff half my trust fund for a 2.1 in PPE from Balliol to be a bloody worker drone. Anyhow, my dealer, Hugo, told me that there was a safe seat up for grabs in some grubby corner of the provinces - and I thought 'Why the bloody hell not?'"*

DOCTORS

Healthcare is probably the only profession where we can all agree that you can be excused for being a bit of a cunt most of the time. No-one who spends the bulk of their time dealing with injured, sick and dying people can be blamed if all of that grimness rubs off on them to some extent.

So it is all the more surprising that doctors are almost universally decent, professional people who use their time to try and make the world a better and healthier place. With this being the case, it is probably only polite to overlook the very occasional mass murderer that emerges from their ranks.

NURSES

Kind, lovely, caring people - who I refuse to criticise in any way.

Except for their terrible, terrible taste in music.

FIRE & RESCUE

Selfless heroes who literally run into harm's way to save the rest of us when we do something really stupid or get caught up in dangerously unfortunate circumstances.

This being the case it is probably not fair ro mention the fact that they are all chronically addicted to internet pornography.

THE POLICE

It looks like no fun at all and everyone hates you. Just why the fuck would anyone want to join the police?

An unofficial, wide ranging survey[S] across thousands of officers in the UK carried out in the mid 2010s revealed the five most popular reasons:

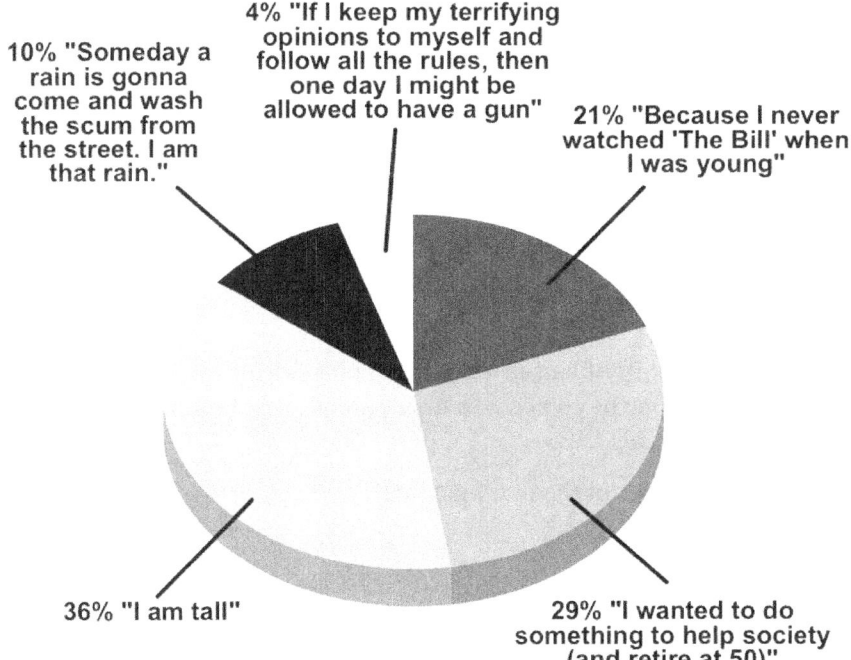

10% "Someday a rain is gonna come and wash the scum from the street. I am that rain."

4% "If I keep my terrifying opinions to myself and follow all the rules, then one day I might be allowed to have a gun"

21% "Because I never watched 'The Bill' when I was young"

36% "I am tall"

29% "I wanted to do something to help society (and retire at 50)"

[S] "About You - About Me - About Us", Police Information Gazette, 2014

COMMUNITY SUPPORT OFFICERS

Considering the kind of people that are allowed to be police officers these days, you've really got to wonder just what is wrong with the ones who end up being 'Community Support Officers'.

Hated just as much as the normal Police, but having none of the 'he just fell down the stairs' powers to go with it, they must be deeply masochistic, incredibly naive, or maybe just in need of a fresh change of clothes that they didn't have to pay for.

You'd think that supporting the community would involve things like dealing with anti-social behaviour, helping with crime prevention issues and providing a reassuring presence for local residents. Apparently not. It seems that the preferred M.O. of your local C.S.O. is to stroll from coffee shop to coffee shop, pushing into queues and artlessly chatting up the awkward girl being the counter who is still young enough to be impressed or intimidated by someone in uniform.

If you try to interrupt them to inform them about a nearby shoplifting, mugging or bank robbery they will rapidly deploy all of their skills, training and experience to phone the actual Police to come and sort it out.

Of course give them a crime petty enough and watch them fling down the coconut latte they just managed to blag from Nero's and vault across car bonnets in full on Dirty Harry mode to apprehend a little old lady who just accidentally dropped a tissue in the street.

After a long hard shift of half-price coffees, one-sided flirting and OAP intimidation, it's time to go home to their parent's spare room to rub one out over a taser catalogue.

Truly the thinnest part of the thin blue line.

PROBATION

The ideal probation officer:

A tough but fair, no nonsense, hard as nails, black belt, former gang member turned criminology Phd. Someone who combines the wisdom of the streets with a firm grasp of the science and practice of criminal rehabilitation.

The real world probation officer:

A pale vegan called Nigel, who grew up in an off-grid yurt community in Devon, has a B.A in Peace Studies and lists his hobbies as 'Anarcho Composting' and 'Jazz Didgeridoo'.

TRAFFIC WARDENS

Twelve awful jobs that are still better than being a traffic warden:

1. Colonic Irrigation Technician

2. Cricket Box Tester

3. Crocodile Enclosure Cleaner

4. The Person That Cleans The Bird Shit Off Nelson's Column

5. Ryanair Food Taster

6. Sewer Fatburg Melter

7. Giraffe Inseminator

8. Hospital Waste Recycler

9. Facebook Content Moderator (only just)

10. Prison Podiatrist

11. Wedding DJ

12. Donkey Gelder

THE TRADES

A PLAGUE OF TEETH SUCKING EXTORTIONISTS

BUILDERS

Any construction site is home to a wide variety of skilled and experienced contractors - there will also be some builders there. Here are the key types to keep an eye out for:

The 'Full-Fat Coke Break'

This proud specimen will be shirtless as soon as the temperature is above twelve degrees and it isn't raining too heavily. Labours under the misapprehension that their spongy, back-hair enhanced torso is inspiring all sorts of erotic reveries in nearby office workers. The truth is that the only people aroused by their slack man-boobs and gammon-like arms are any cannibalistic serial killers who happen to be attending an accountancy seminar nearby.

The 'Dead-Eyed Workhorse'

A sad, pale tired looking individual who, due to their immigration status or lack of experience, is the one who actually has to do all the work. Often a bundle of wiry strength and twitchy aggression due to the long days of fetching and carrying fuelled only by petrol station sausage rolls and two cans of budget energy drink an hour. Almost certainly dealing drugs on the side, mostly to help support their drug habit.

The 'Self-Described Ladies' Man'

Society's most vile and aggressive misogynistic abusers... can only dream of reaching the plateau of female unease caused by these construction site cat-calling bastards. When not ruining some poor woman's day with snarling, unwanted scaffold-based propositions, they indulge in practical hobbies such as chloroform home-brewing, van soundproofing and secret basement improvement.

They like to give the false impression that they may have been in the forces, take aggressive patriotism to fetishistic heights and always order chips in Indian restaurants - basically, The Sun newspaper in human form.

The 'Angry Inconveniencer'

A moody specialist. You will never see one of these gruff individuals so much as lift a trowel or move a brick. When someone is needed to park a van across your driveway, or glare at you as you wait in your car while a construction lorry does an hour-long three point turn on the high street at rush hour - they come into their own. By deploying the kind of intimidating presence that late 80's Mike Tyson would cross a busy road to avoid, they allow the construction industry to get away with shit that the rest of us would get beaten up or fined for.

PLUMBERS

In recent years, there has been a huge growth in plumbing services provided by women to women. If you are a male plumber then what do you think the popularity of such services says about you?

For the avoidance of doubt what it says is:

"Everyone thinks that you are probably a sex pest and wouldn't risk having you in their house even in the middle of a shit spraying, burst-pipe emergency."

The irony of this situation is that sex crime actually plays second fiddle to a plumber's main criminal intent - extorting as much money out you with the smallest amount of effort. It starts with the exorbitant 'emergency call out fee' which somehow classes 2pm on a Wednesday afternoon as unsociable working hours. On arrival, your problem will not be fixed until a few simple, but deceptively subtle, questions establish how plumbing savvy you are and therefore just how much they can take the piss. If they think you might know one end of a tap spanner from the other, then they will miserably fix the problem, taking as long as humanly possible in order to charge as much as they can. If you a clearly a mark, then a pantomime of teeth sucking and exasperated sighing will lead to a point where they turn the water supply off, mumble something about not having the right kind of tool in the van and arrange to come back and fix things properly some time tomorrow, which will cost you even more money.

When you actually get to see a plumber doing some work, take a moment to admire the two genuine skills inherent in all those in the industry:

A) Not being bothered at all by the smell of shit.

B) Being able to kneel down at just the right angle to make it almost impossibly hard to see the electronic tag on their ankle.

ELECTRICIANS

There are certain people, who in the course of their work, literally have your life in their hands. You expect these people to be competent, thoughtful and highly trained. Think of the times you may have seen an airline pilot or a heart surgeon - they will be confident, reassuring and highly reliable.

Now think about the tired-looking, clearly hungover geezer that came round to put in your new fusebox. His work will have a far larger impact on the continued survival of yourself and your family - and you paid him in cash to help him avoid the paperwork and save you a few quid. Now whenever the washing machine reaches the climax of its spin cycle the lights in your house start to flicker and a faint smell of burning fills the air.

For some reason, electricians are known as 'Sparks' in the trade. Like a fucking spark is something you ever want to see when dealing with electricity. It is the equivalent of calling a bus driver a 'Crash'.

ARCHITECTS

The ideal profession for someone who wants to give the impression of rugged practicality by occasionally wearing work boots and a hard hat, but has no desire to get their hands dirty, listen to a screetchy radio all day or shout abuse at passing women.

Astoundingly, it takes about the same amount of time to train as an architect as it does to become a medical doctor. Seven years spent neatly arranging expensive drawing equipment, memorising the 'extras' list on the Audi website, shouting abuse at the screen while watching Grand Designs and dropping Le Corbusier into every fucking conversation they ever have.

Once qualified they spend most of their time 'architecting' the construction of those dull prefabricated industrial units, or charging rich idiots a fortune to 'design' house extensions using Sketchup templates that cost them a tenner.

To be fair, they need to make as much money as possible while the sun is shining on their particular grift. Once the world realises that the average nine year old kid with two months Minecraft experience is capable of designing far more elegant, sustainable and practical structures than most trained professionals, the game will be up.

INTERIOR DESIGNERS

All across our world there are people engaged in dangerous humanitarian missions. People risking life and limb amid war zones, famines and natural disasters, often relying on charitable donations to keep a (canvas) roof over their head and surviving on basic rations.

Only a few time zones away there are people who get paid six figures to choose which shade of hot pink an investment banker's fourth bathroom should be.

Every day that an interior designer gets through without committing suicide out of sheer embarrassment is an achievement. They are the term 'first world problems' made flesh.

In their own way they do risk actual bodily harm on a regular basis by walking into half decorated rooms full of contractors and having hissy fits because the hinges on the bespoke cupboards are the wrong type of distressed zinc. How more of them don't end up victims of sudden hammer rage is a bit of a mystery.

PAINTERS/DECORATORS

Your ideal job would be a cool art teacher that all the kids get on with, but your 'possession with intent to supply' lifestyle means that leading the art therapy class on F wing is as near as you'll ever get to a school.

So instead you set yourself up in the one field where you can justifiably inhale solvents all day, while you slap a bit of Magnolia on some old dear's bathroom walls in exchange for £50 cash in hand.

The other key benefit of this particular trade is that the smell of all the paint, thinners and wallpaper glue masks the scent of the unpleasant skunk that you deal out of the back of your deeply sinister van.

LANDSCAPE GARDENERS

Never, ever - and I can't really emphasise this strongly enough - look inside their composting bin.

Enough said.

CAR MECHANICS

What film franchise comes to mind when you think of the oily, sweaty world of car workshops and mechanics? Maybe The Fast and Furious, or possibly Mad Max? The right answer is in fact, Toy Story.

In the Toy Story films, the toys are always up to all sorts of fun and adventures, right up until a person appears, then they all stop what they are doing and become inanimate objects.

The exact same thing happens in any modern garage, but in reverse. While any customer is within ear or eyeshot the scene will be a noisy, shouty, clanging affair, with cars being raised, wrenches wrenched, sticks dipped and throttles revved. Once no-one is around they drop the pretence, plug a laptop into the USB socket on the engine and then quietly and calmly follow the instructions on the screen.

Why the act you may well ask? Well, if everyone realised that fixing cars wasn't a matter of complex mechanical skills and years of experience, but was in fact a case of having a USB cable and a working internet connection then there would suddenly be a lot of mechanics working in other jobs. That may not sound like a big issue, but think of the practical implications...

- You order a burger, the bloke at the counter shakes his head and sighs, "No chance mate, I can't get the parts in until next Wednesday".

- You buy two tickets at the cinema, the bloke behind the counter sucks his teeth, tells you that "it's a much bigger job that we thought", then charges you £12 for the tickets and £79.99 for labour.

- Your laptop is playing up and you take it in to be fixed. You are shocked to learn that it will take a whole week, but glad to learn that they can loan you another device to tide you over. It is a 1995 solar powered pocket calculator, with the multiplication button missing and a load of sellotape holding the back on. You have to show them your passport before they let you take it away.

Best to keep them exactly where they are really.

THE ARTS

TWATTING ABOUT WHILE
YOUR PARENTS PAY THE RENT

ACTORS

Getting paid for dressing up and playing make pretend may sound like fun, but acting is a tough gig. Well, it's a tough gig if you're not from a wealthy family who can afford to pay your rent until your old school ties or showbiz family connections get you some decent work.

Don't believe all the bollocks you might hear spouted about 'finding the character' or 'the truth of the piece'. The quality of any performance on film, TV or the stage is now purely judged by the amount of weight/muscle gained or lost by the performer in question. The most poorly judged, wooden performance will win a bucket of awards if an actor eats a bucket of KFC every day for six months in order to become 'unrecognisable' for a dark, violent re-boot of Humpty Dumpty.

Due to all the attention they get and the bizarre amount of money they get paid, famous actors are by some distance the profession which has the widest possible disparity between:
- How useful and important they are for society
- How useful and important they think they are for society

It is a strange state of affairs when we are getting sternly lectured on political matters by some self-important, over muscled, trust fund case who spends most of their life in front of a green screen, shouting at a tennis ball on a stick.

The best 'acting' you'll see is the Hollywood star feigning shock, anger and sadness when yet another instance of racial prejudice, sexual abuse or financial corruption emerges from tinseltown. They seem genuinely surprised that an industry prepared to pay them tens millions of dollars for looking pretty and occasionally doing a dodgy accent is somehow not completely on the level.

MUSICIANS

According to people who study these things, it takes ten-thousand hours to get really good at playing a musical instrument. That's about ten years of painstaking, dedicated practice and learning - all so you can annoy the shit out of the general public with your ground-breaking, solo acoustic interpretation of Jay Z's '99 Problems' at the local open mic night.

All those thousands of hours prioritised towards honing their musical skills means that many musicians run something of a deficit in other life skills that most of us take for granted - not acting like a spoiled child is one, understanding how money works is another. In fact the wise thing to do is to subtract those ten years from any musician's actual age to get a clear picture of their mental age and general competency at life.

The ninetenn year old pop sensation, who constantly moans about the 'slavery' of the multi-million pound contract that she signed last year has the self-awareness of a nine year old and had the legal understanding of an eight year old when she agreed the contract.

That twenty-four year old singer who won some talent show, then went mad and spent all his new money on drugs and prostitutes, is really a hormone ravaged teenage show-off who has just been given half a million quid.

The thirty-six year old rock band guitarist is twenty-six in his head - hence the attempt to maintain artfully unkempt long hair despite the onset of male pattern baldness. The skinny jeans and ironic, too-tight t-shirts exacerbate the growing paunch, while undiagnosed type 2 diabetes means that maintaining the rock and roll lifestyle is punishingly hard work.

If you don't have the good sense to split up the band before you hit thirty then prepare to look like a mid-career undercover cop trying to infiltrate a teen skate gang.

VIDEO GAME DEVELOPERS

Not nearly as clever as they think they are. These naive fools have been tricked into thinking that rather than being trapped in an abusive, demanding and notoriously anti workers rights industry, their job is cool and fun, all because they can wear trainers to work and there is an old pinball machine in the office.

When out in public they gather in groups, taking up a whole table in your local pub to spend the evening playing an insanely complicated board game, which will be called something like 'Battle Cry of the Cybermage Dragons'. They will insist that the music in the pub is turned down and drink tap water all night. Listen in and amongst the Cybermage Dragon chatter, you'll hear hot takes on which is the best Pokemon, news on the latest trends in involuntary celibacy and disagreements on exactly how to pronounce 'Ayn Rand'.

Back home they will spend the early hours posting ironically unironic anti-immigrant memes onto web message boards under the pseudonym 'EdgeLORD_Himmler_X', before knocking one out over the hidden camera footage of the Polish lady who comes to clean the office.

Weekends are usually spent at work doing unpaid overtime, trying to find more efficient ways to get twelve year old kids helplessly addicted to new and subtle forms of cartoonish gambling.

If they do end up at a loose end, then they can probably be found re-arranging their collection of boxed and pristine anime action figures into order of value - while their parents have deliberately noisy sex in the next room.

THE FILM INDUSTRY

The glitzy and horrifically exploitative world of movie making is known for using strange, old-timey slang terms for 'behind the scenes' jobs.

While your average pub quiz team could tell you that the chief electrician is known as the 'Gaffer' and that a 'Dolly Grip' is someone that pushes the camera around, there are many more film industry job titles that you've probably never heard of...

'Tin Jockey' Creative production executive tasked with screwing money out of rich, stupid people in exchange for a 'Co-Executive Producer' credit on IMDB, plus an awkward photo with one of the third-tier actors from the direct-to-streaming horror film they are filming as part of a complicated tax credit fraud.

'Friendly Hector' A junior technician in the construction department with additional on-set responsibility for manually inserting cocaine right up the director's arsehole.

'Box Otter' The senior executive responsible for hourly monitoring and physical enforcement measures related to the weight of female on-screen talent. Named after the pre-war medical practice of feeding raw Otter testicles to young women for '*the prevention of matronly tendencies and worldly female hysterias*'.

'Hefty Laddie' Male star's naked stand in / 'Personal Assistant'.

'Smoky Chainlocker' Supervisor responsible for the distribution of all production funds related to sexual harassment claims and their associated Non Disclosure Agreements.

'Paisley Figwhacker' Sound effect specialist responsible for any and all sounds related to bodily functions. Named after a technique used in European arthouse cinema during the 1970s.

'Nudgebill Screw' Artist in charge of removing non-white cast members from promotional materials.

'Daddy Pot Pot' The acting coach placed in charge of coaxing the required performance from babies and small children. Union rules mean that they must operate under the strict 'Uppity Child Enwranglement Procedures' first ratified by the industry in 1932 and updated in 1975 by a special panel of feature directors, co-chaired by Roman Polanski and Woody Allen.

'Duff Tyke' Breast and cleavage lighting supervisor.

'Junior Heckswab' Assistant in charge of cleaning up any animal corpses resulting from production activities on or off the set.

'Popular Jeffrey' On-set doctor, pharmacist, passport forger and pimp.

'Drop Hand' Specialist role responsible for coming up with and executing all of the hilarious, escalating pranks that superstar actors like to play on each other, but don't have the wit to think up or the ingenuity to carry out. On 'Oceans 12' the Drop Hand budget was twice the size of that for production design.

'Agente Au Nationale' Executive producer in charge of maximising product placement revenue.

'Glasgow Tightener' Executive producer's personal abortionist.

'Jazzboy' Responsible for bribing journalists, reviewers and bloggers in order to get positive media attention and glowing reviews for some grindingly dull comic book sequel about a nerdy librarian who gets super powers after being bitten by a genetically altered Shitzu.

'Swing Miser' Emergency teeth whitener and eyebrow shaper.

'Stuffed Albert' Continuity supervisor responsible for monitoring exactly how many times a character has blinked in any given scene.

'Brookstrong' A stunt performer who specialises in being puched, kicked, or otherwise struck in the groin. Named after famed New England bodybuilder and involuntary eunoch Howie J. Brookstrong.

'Powder Fanny' Organised crime liason and car valet supervisor.

'Gallop Marker' Lead arse-crack waxing technician.

'Congleton' Publicist in charge of leaking stories to the press about how much secret work all the actors involved in the production do for charity.

'Enfield' Old school role, still kept as a tradition on many modern productions. A technician responsible for stencilling job titles and names on those folding canvas chairs. Fun fact: A young Lars von Trier worked as the Enfield on The King of Comedy.

GRAPHIC DESIGNERS

A day in the life of successful graphic designer, Tristan X. Barnes, 34.

06.30: Woken by the sound of classic era Kraftwerk coming from my Bose bedroom system. Check news and messages on my phone.

06.40: Twenty minutes on my maple wood pilates reformer.

07.00: Shower, shave with antique cut-throat razor, apply a variety of Tom Ford toiletries.

07.30: Dress in dark graphite Zilli suit over a plain black D&G shirt, choose the TAG chronograph watch from the wall safe.

07.45: Eggs Royale for breakfast.

8.10: Weather is bad, so roof up on the Maserati as I head to the office.

8.40: Arrive at work, espresso, flick through Creative Review, check emails and billing figures on my triple-monitored Mac Pro.

9.30: Weekly meeting with the team working on the Anderson account, agree that pale blue is the way to go. Bill the client £600 for my time.

10.00: Client meeting with a major credit card company, they need to make T&Cs as hard to read as possible while staying within legal limits. Recommend a custom font designed for minimum legibility.

12.00: Lunch at sushi bar with clients.

13.30: Squash with Roger, a partner at Hogginton, Jellsworth & Kline, I win comfortably and we discuss the potential takeover of the firm in the showers.

15.30: Back to the office to purchase some ready made templates we will pass off as our own work to one of our less valuable clients next week.

16.30: Drive to a nearby industrial estate. Park outside a unit with no signage.

16.35: Use a shiny black and red keycard to gain access to the unit via a side door. Enter a reception area painted stark white, with what looks like a pentagram marked out in blood red on the floor. "What is your pleasure, Mr Barnes?"asks a female voice over an unseen intercom. "Number four, please." I reply. There is an almost imperceptible click as a door slides open and I walk through. A terrified young man, gagged and clearly drugged, is chained to an antique dentist' chair, a tray of stainless steel medical implements sits on a table to one side. The door slides shut behind me.

18.30: Arrive home, a few lengths of the pool. Slip into Boss loungewear.

19.00: Light dinner in front of my huge B&O TV, watching some German New Wave via the BFI player.

21.00: Two hours of Playstation or 4Chan, then bed.

ARTISTS

Artists will tell you that 'Art' is subjective and as such transcends traditional measures of value, taste and skill. Until they come to sell it, then the value of everything becomes very measurably objective.

The six artworks described below all sold at auction for more than $1 million. One of them is made up, can you guess which?

My Ex, Machine 'A' (1998)

Sold for $2.3M in 2007

A solid gold cast of a vibrator, with a signed Polaroid photo of Burt Reynolds fixed to it with masking tape.

Trust, but verify (2001)

Sold for $1.2M in 2006

100 A4 photocopies of 1980s adverts for photocopiers, mounted on a large plywood board, rested on two vintage office chairs.

Mogadishu (1989)

Sold for $3.1M in 2015

Looped eight minute VHS video of the artist, dressed as Nancy Reagan, silently reading a paperback edition of The Naked Lunch.

Two Parallel Lines Meet (2016)

Sold for $1.7M in 2016

A two metre tall reproduction of the credit card receipt for the artist's purchase of a €120,000 Porsche. The image is made up of thousands of smaller versions of itself.

Come Together (2001)

Sold for $4M in 2010

A Nescafe coffee (label intact) containing the ashes of the artist's parents, suspended by barbed wire above a scale model of the Vatican.

Untitled (2002)

Sold for $12M in 2019

Five foot tall fibreglass sculpture of Donald Duck being crucified.

MEDIA

VACANT SHIT-STIRRERS, CORPORATE SHILLS AND RIGHT WING MANIACS

INFLUENCERS

We can't say we weren't warned.

When the term 'Reality TV Star' entered popular usage, we should have all had a long hard think about what that said about our shared cultural landscape and resolved to try much harder.

When a sizable proportion of people started taking photos of their meals and posting them on the internet, we should have recognised the direction that things were heading in and done something about it. Something decisive and appropriately harsh.

When it turned out that sharing pictures of your arse and publicly acting like a spoiled toddler all of the time was a way of becoming a billionaire, our leaders should have stepped in, taken responsibility and turned everything off.

In ignoring these warning signs,a rubicon was crossed - a vacuous, airbrushed rubicon - sending us hurtling inexorably towards the terminal-stage, crapitalist twatocracy that we find ourselves inhabiting. A world where 'Tripadvisor Top Reviewer' is an actual career goal rather than a cruel insult. A society where absolutely nothing is considered too trashy, embarrassing or unethical for those trying to get on the influencer gravy train. A culture who values the possession of a thigh gap above possession of a Nobel prize.

The sad part about the influencer game is that those at the top of the tree, with legions of followers, were born stinking rich anyway. Getting paid a million quid to flash their boobs near a KFC logo is probably entirely inconsequential to them - just another gold-plated Ferrari to gather dust in the garage, while they consider the competing bids to name their kid 'Pfizer' or 'Starbucks'.

There's a common thought experiment about going back in time and killing Hitler to prevent the horrors he perpetrated. Swinging by the nascent Facebook server room with a baseball bat on the way back through the time tunnel might not be a bad idea either.

THE PRESS

It is genuinely hard to think of a profession that has fallen further from grace in recent history than journalism.

It is hilarious to think that the free press was once considered a vital pillar of democracy, relied upon to hold the powerful to account and expose the corrupt and unethical. These days the collective efforts of the fourth estate mostly consist of copying and pasting banal celebrity pronouncements from Twitter and taking every possible step to dumb down the quality of public discourse to the level of a spoiled baby.

Much is made of maintaining the freedom of the press - an idea which sounds great if the 'press' is a noble, upstanding seeker of truth and defender of the public's right to know what those in charge are up to. It seems less ideal when it is used as a protection for looking up skirts, publishing spurious gossip about eating disorders and bullying people to near suicide because they possibly got fingered by a footballer in Ayia Napa.

You don't need to be a mad conspiracy theorist to be concerned that most of our news media is owned and managed by a decreasingly small circle of bitter billionaires. A cabal of crusty, greedy, corrupt old geezers who have complete editorial control and more axes to grind than a Viking blacksmith.

NEWS JOURNALISTS

To be a successful news reporter you need a wide range of stalking skills.

Creepy 'Catfish' style social media stalking, where despite the fact that you are a 43 year old male alcoholic named Terry, you pretend to be 'Becki' a 14 year old girl who in turn is masquerading as a buxom 20 year old aspiring model called 'Aspen'. All in an ongoing attempt to get dick pics from someone in the House of Lords.

You'll also need some determined and shameless real world stalking skills, in order track down the friends and family of someone who dared to call the queen 'an old bitch' on a drunken facebook post eight years ago.

You threaten all involved with inclusion in the story until you track down the offender to their house where you repeatedly question why they hate their country through the letterbox and then lay siege to their house for days.

Eventually you'll starve them out for a walk of shame to the shops while you yell questions at them and get an old ex-soldier with all his medals on to appear in the photos looking sad.

Finally you'll also need some high-tech phone cracking and password guessing experience for the completely justifiable public interest investigation into the personal messages and photos exchanged privately between some geezer who was on Britain's Got Talent for five minutes and his secret ex boyfriend.

Of course, most of the news you'll actually end up working on is clickbait articles for the web with titles like, '10 Ways That Love Island Shook Us And Gave Us All The Feels'.

COLUMNISTS

The pinnacle of the whole journalism game, a job that involves shitting out 1000 words of horribly out of touch opinion once a week - and somehow getting paid six figures for the effort. As well as being a cushy gig it is also remarkably secure, as long as you don't get caught interfering with animals or accidentally fail upwards into the role of Prime Minister, then you are pretty much set for life.

Your approach will probably depend on your political alignment, albeit to a cartoonishly extreme degree. A newspaper column is a platform for the kind of views and opinions that would get most people instantly sacked, justifiably shunned or soundly beaten. Whichever end of the political see-saw they are perched on, a newspaper columnist is basically an internet troll with a spectacular expense account.

In addition to the crypto-fascist nutters and whiney wannabe radicals there are also a bunch of celebrity columnists, consisting mainly of:

Retired sportsmen (ideally those considered 'a bit of a character' in their playing days, but without any domestic violence convictions) who are paid for sticking their gurning face over articles knocked up by the office intern following a strict no words with more than two syllables mandate.

Washed-up comedians who dump all their failed material into their column with the occasional topical name or reference thrown in to make it seem vaguely relevant.

BROADCAST JOURNALISTS

Like a skinhead England fan singing, "Two world wars and one world cup", these well-groomed Oxbridge media whores live off the past glories of their profession.

Life as a TV journalist used to be about heading to the troublespots of the world, bunkering down in the last hotel in town and drinking yourself to death while notifying the outside world about some genocidal civil war or other.

Thankfully the internet (along with modern health and safety policies that extend further than a bag full of free Campari and penicillin) has now removed the need for some alcoholic toff to go and posh-splain the problems of the world on location. This has left broadcast journalists free to focus on more domestic issues - and by domestic issues I mean:

- Waiting around outside houses and then appearing live on the news to explain that they are waiting around outside a house.
- Desperately trying not to use the first name, or nickname of any politician that they shared a flat with at uni with or were at a car-key party with the other night.
- Occasionally getting the nerve up to yell, "Are you going to resign, Minister?" across Downing Street, but from within a crowd to mask their identity.
-Turning up to the scene of any disaster in full hazmat gear or bullet proof vest, collaring some poor bastard whose house has just burnt down, floated away or blown up and enquiring, "Can you tell us what you are feeling right now?"

One enduring mystery surrounding all broadcast journalists, is 'Why the fuck do they talk like that?'

It has been almost 20 years since satires like The Day Today lampooned the ridiculous vocal intonation and emphasis used by TV news readers and reporters. Strangely this just made them all double down to the point where even the most basic soundbite comes across like William Shatner doing a Harold Pinter play while having a stroke.

"The Home Secretary... seen today openinganewprisoninReading... has denied the reports linking him... TO THE SCANDAL involving payments to

several prostitutes. The PRIME MINSTER'S view of this grooowwwwiinngg scandal will. Be. Crucial. Back to you… in the studio… David."

The only ray of sunshine in any 'piece to camera' is when a heroic member of the public takes it upon themselves to subvert the whole medium by being as distracting as possible in the background by pulling faces, making 'wanker' gestures or holding up some kind of obscene handwritten message.

A select few that have served their time in the field, don't have a string of drink-driving convictions and are good at pronouncing difficult words will progress into the coveted 'back in the studio', presenter roles. Here they will gradually evolve into a preening caricature of themselves and develop an aggressive and pedantic bad cop/worse cop interviewing technique, intended to belittle and taunt without extracting any meaningful information at all.

YOUTUBERS/STREAMERS

In the mid-1800s tens of thousands of people abandoned their lives and set out across North America to pursue their dreams of finding Gold. A small number of prospectors had struck lucky and when news reached the rest of the world there was a huge stampede across the continent to try and join the ranks of the super rich. If you already worked in a back breaking manual job (as was common at the time) then why not potentially earn a fortune by doing the same thing prospecting in California?

Of course, only very few realised their dreams, the vast majority were ripped off, contracted TB or cholera, suffered fatal attacks from native Americans or got stabbed by Ian McShane in a saloon. The people who got really rich were the ones who sold the prospecting equipment and ran the brothels.

Around 2010, millions of people abandoned all self awareness and started putting videos of themselves on the internet. It appeared that by filming or live-streaming themselves playing video games, talking complete bollocks or having a wank, some pioneers had already struck it rich. Those who already spent most of their time playing games, talking shite and masturbating thought they might as well get paid to do it.

Of course only a very few people realised their dreams, most ended up struggling to pay the rent while dealing with vitamin D deficiencies, carpal tunnel syndrome and horrendous mental health issues. The people who got really rich were YouTube, Twitch, Pornhub and anyone with shares in companies that made webcams, sex toys or anti-depressants.

BLOGGERS

To: **manager@grrbistro.com**
From: **pips@flirtyfoodiefilly.co.uk**
Subject: **A visit from the Flirty Foodie Filly!!**

Hey Graham!

My name is Pippa, you've probably heard of my 'Flirty Foodie Filly' blog, I've been hearing grrrrreat things about your esteemed establishment and I'd love to come and do a review! It's my hubby's bday on Thursday the 19th, so I thought that might be an ideal opportunity to come and check you guys out!!

If you could arrange a tasting menu of your main dishes and a couple of wines that would be fine - I don't charge for doing reviews even though my blog gets over a thousand views a week and was featured in mumsnets 'Hot 500 local food divas 2017'. We will need our food and drink to be complementary (obvs!!) as well as a taxi to and fro (I don't want to put any ideas in your head but a birthday cake for my man wouldn't go amiss!!??!!).

TTFN !!

Pippa

To: **manager@grrbistro.com**
From: **pips@flirtyfoodiefilly.co.uk**
Subject: **Bella's in da house!!!!!**

Greetings Mr Graham!

Just wanted to let you know that my gal-pal Arrabella - aka 'Buxom Bella the Vino Vixen' aka @BustyVino of world renowned Instagram fame is going to be joining us on the 19th, along with her 'significant other', Deano. So if we'll need food for 4 and do make sure you have some bad ass bottles from your cellar lined up for her Bella-ness (she loves a Sancerre) - that would be just fab. We'll be with you some time between 6 and 9 - I haven't heard back so just to confirm I'll book the taxi, but will need cash reimbursement on arrival. Any probs let me know???!

Seeya!

The Pipster

PS if you want Bella to do any Insta posts at your place, she charges £25 for a standard shot and £50 quid for her classic "Downblouse Wine Sip" pose. She'll need the money the day before.

To: **manager@grrbistro.com**
From: **pips@flirtyfoodiefilly.co.uk**
Subject: **I'VE NEVER BEEN SO INSULTED IN MY LIFE**

ONE: Your so-called staff had no record of our booking when we arrived, they didn't even seem to know who we were. I was EMBARRASSED for them. A lot of your other customers seemed embarrassed about the whole scene too!

TWO: We were told that we would have to WAIT for a table like we were normal customers. At this point I informed the waiter (Tim) that our nanny, Jemma, has a grandmother from Jamaica, so he needed to check his white privilege and get us a table straight away. Tim told us that made no sense - because we are white and he just happened to be black - I tried to educate him about systemic racism but he said something about having a degree in African Studies, in what we all felt was a very impolite manner. Bella was especially upset as she has been to the Notting Hill Carnival on several occasions.

THREE: I immediately demanded to see you to sort this whole mess out - only to learn that you were elsewhere, due to what we were told were 'Family reasons'. You knew we were coming last week couldn't your family re-arrange their reasons? UNPROFESSIONAL!!!

FOUR: We were given menus!!??!! Tim said he knew nothing about a tasting menu being arranged! All my followers know that I have decision related anxiety and IBS issues - so being forced to read a menu is literally a health and safety issue for me.

FIVE: Although we did announce our terms clearly to our fellow diners upon arrival, no-one was willing to respect our safe space. Several of your 'patrons' forcefully requested that we stop taking photos and videos of them, even having the nerve to suggest that we somehow needed their permission! Tim even had the nerve to tell us that Deano couldn't play us his latest Ibiza Massive Mix while we ate - he'd bought his new 200 Watt bluetooth speaker specially for it too.

SIX: After our meal, Tim presented us with a bill!!!??? I, of course ignored this - but as we were leaving, a group of your staff blocked our way and refused to move until we had paid them. I explained that as a reviewer my food and drink was obviously complementary - Tim said that he had no idea what we were talking about and then just because Bella made an obviously ironic joke about 'coming back to burn you all out' he then phoned the police. The cheers of your other customers as the officers led us away clearly showed that they supported us in our stand against your FASCIST establishment.

You've left me no option but to use my skills as a journalist and platform as a strong independent woman to raise awareness of your toxic establishment. I have posted a one star review on tripadvisor with the heading 'Expensive Steaks with side order of RACISM' and will be giving you a 'Flirty Filly Fumbs Down' rating on my site.

Be under no illusion, you will be hearing from my father's lawyer about this.

Ms Phillipa Dovington-Hillsop (BA Hons)

OTHER

TOO SHIT TO FIT IN A PROPER CATEGORY

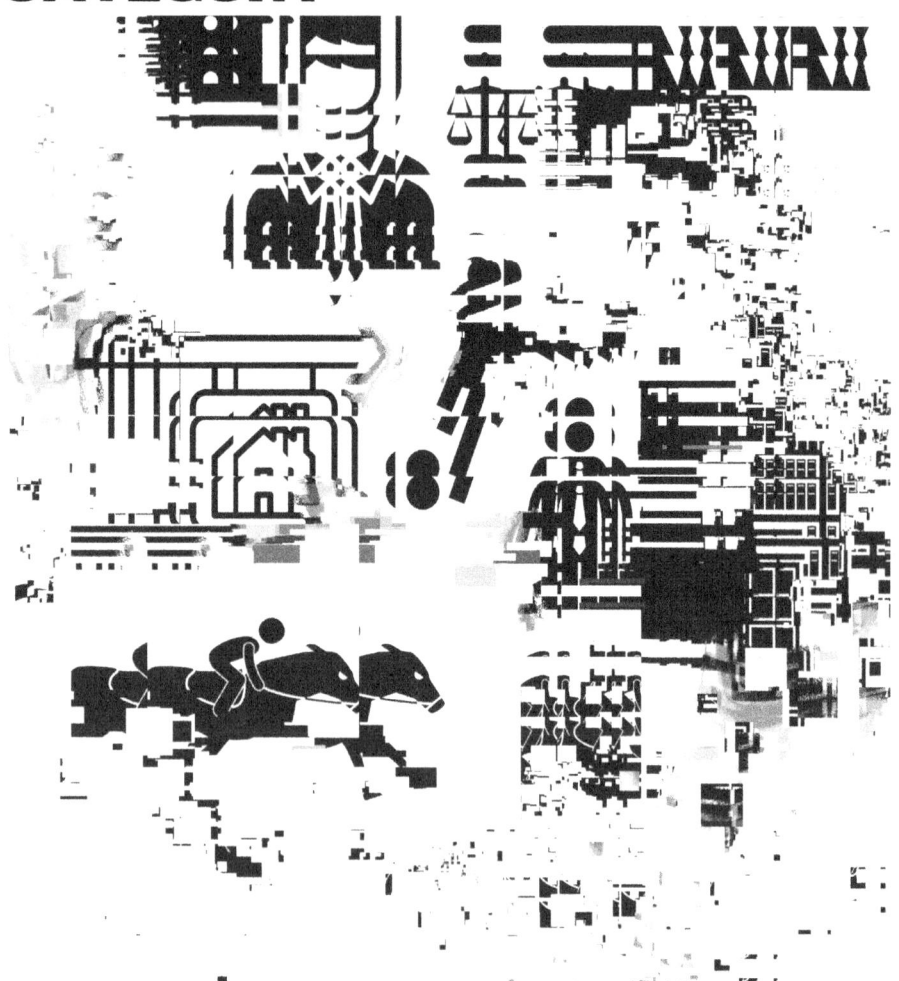

SOLICITORS

In his most famous work, The Trial, Franz Kafka helped create the view of the legal system as an impenetrable enigma.

Society as a legal construct is a complex and potentially malignant machine that we are trapped within but without the knowledge or agency to influence the workings of the machine or the effect that it has on our lives.

This being the case, even the most modest legal professionals weld an almost arcane power over us, a power conferred by years of training in the centuries of tradition and layers of protocol and procedure too complicated for the average person to even hope to negotiate.

But basically, they charge you an arm and a leg to fill in forms that you could easily complete yourself, then invoice you £20 for the fucking stamp they put on the envelope. The shameless wankers.

It turns out that solicitors are one of the professions most at risk from the rising tide of algorithmic automation in the workplace. You can train a computer to follow basic legal procedures with zero errors far more easily than you can train one to do something manual, like clean a toilet.

So in five year's time when you've had a particularly messy and explosive dump in a public toilet, don't feel guilty. The chap who failed to warn you that your new house was built on a former uranium mine - but still invoiced you for a grand anyway - will be along shortly.

Justice is both blind and ironic it seems.

ESTATE AGENTS

The BMW M3 is a rare and expensive car. It has been precisely designed and engineered for high speed maneuvering around the Nurburgring circuit in the hands of expert racing drivers, who drag every ounce of performance out of its huge engine and finely balanced chassis.

Away from the track, preening idiots with names like 'Milo' use them to drive an average of 8 miles a day at a top speed of 29 miles per hour, then leave them on double yellow lines outside some semi-condemned, asbestos ridden hovel that they are trying to pass off as 'an ideal investment opportunity'.

The main reason that estate agents choose to drive overpowered, limited edition cars such as the M3 is that they can't quite afford a Porsche yet.

In general estate agents are a bit like the human appendix. An estate agent performs no useful function and theoretically we could all exist happily without them. Despite this, we have no choice but to be stuck with them, knowing that they are mostly known for causing painful emergencies. Even recruitment consultants look down on estate agents.

If the outlandish plot of 'The Purge' films was enacted and for 24 hours and everyone could murder anyone without any risk of prosecution, then all the estate agents would be dead within half an hour.

LETTING AGENTS

In the theoretical purge scenario outlined opposite, estate agents would only last half an hour because everyone would be turning their violent attentions to letting agents first as a matter of urgent priority.

To be successful as a letting agent you need a strange and rather counterintuitive set of personality traits.

First, you must have a zealous desire to enforce every tiny single little rule, no matter how pointless or unpleasant:

"As the kitchen door wasn't left open at an angle of exactly 37 degrees after you vacated the premises we are not required by law to return your security deposit. We'll be invoicing you for the service charge this incurs."

Second, you must have, let's call it, the moral flexibility to screw as much money as possible out of people who are in no position to do anything but comply:

"Oh, didn't Kevin tell you about the key handover signing charge? I'll need £100 before I can give you the keys to your new flat - no sorry my mistake - as it is a Wednesday it is £200. No, it has to be cash."

Third, you must lack empathy, compassion and any form of basic human decency to a degree that would make a serial killer blush:

"No, a chemotherapy appointment is not an acceptable reason for missing a routine house inspection. We have no option but to begin eviction proceedings unless you pay the deferred inspection fee, plus service charge, plus VAT. We'll need that by 5pm today... No, it has to be cash."

So what we have here is a bunch of pedantic, extortionist sadists who would probably describe their dream job as 'Death Camp Guard'.

They hate you because you can't afford to buy a house, but they wouldn't have a job if you could. A dismal paradox from which there is no hope of escape.

PROFESSIONAL SPORTS

Football

Half-witted, barely literate, monosyllabic imbeciles who are unable to have sex on their own or drive a car properly.

Rightly considered the absolute scum of the fucking earth while simultaneously being worshipped like living gods. They earn the kind of money that could probably cure cancer and what do they spend it on? Haircuts, ghastly mansions and lawyers.

Turning up at a kid's hospital once a year, in a shell suit with a "Kick Racism Out of Football" badge and a surly demeanour in order to be outwitted at snakes and ladders by a one-eyed eight year-old on a respirator, does not suddenly make you a good person.

You know that kid at school who was really good and had trials at a proper club? He was a complete cock wasn't he?

Horse Racing

Animals are forced to commit incest and the by-products are whipped senseless by a bunch of bulimic, tax dodging midgets right until the end when they clearly let someone else win to keep the bookies happy and rob the proles of their hard earned dosh.

Despite the posh facade, horse racing is also a key destination for angry, aggressive men to drink themselves into oblivion and get into large brawls. This is somehow acceptable as long as their wife/girlfriend is wearing the sort of hat that a blind Las Vegas drag queen would probably consider a bit much.

Truly, the sport of kings.

Golf

Woman-hating middle managers and hopeless showbiz types, all of whom really can't stand the fact that the most successful golfer of all time is black. None of them seem to be able to carry a bag without the assistance of a local peasant or a pointless electric car.

Like the Ku Klux Klan in disgusting diamond patterned sweaters. Oscar Wilde was right about this one.

Tennis

Absolutely sickening – A bunch of spoilt brats that groan like consumptive porn hags at even the most miniscule exertion and then abuse the living shit out of the poor bastards who have given up their weekend to sit and stare at a chalky line on their behalf.

In a recent development it seems they are now incapable of even picking up or putting down a towel, instead they rely on pointing aggressively at small children to get the towel before flinging the sweat sodden item back while demanding "A fucking coke".

Formula One

In-bred European aristocracy, with the occasional suicidal South American, playing follow the leader at 200 mph. The wages push the boundaries of traditional mathematics, while the entertainment on show is limited to who can put petrol in a car quickest.

Hardly ever have the good grace to die in a huge explosion or at least lose a limb in spectacular fashion, despite that being the reason that most people are watching it.

(Side note: Anyone who has 'Big F1 fan' or similar in their twitter bio should be avoided at all costs)

Boxing

Money laundering gangster front involving naïve thugs who don't seem to understand exactly how brain damage is caused.

The most famous fight of all time was won by a man whose entire strategy was to let his opponent beat him senseless until he was really tired – look how that ended up; the winner a victim of crippling Parkinson's disease, the loser a fucking billionaire grill salesman.

Any sport which had Don King as a senior commercial figure is clearly about as honest as a four pound coin.

Athletics

The testing ground for the drugs of tomorrow.

Rugby Union

Attention you blazer-wearing, pint-despoiling, pub-ruiners. I have a message for you:

All the contrived poshness and bizarre team rituals don't disguise the fact that you like to spend Sundays knocking each other around for sadomasochistic kicks.

William Webb Ellis was a cheat who was shit at football, that is the basis of your entire sport.

Rugby League

Physical freaks who labour under the misapprehension that they are better than their union counterparts due to the northern working-class roots of the game. Truth is they aren't sharp enough to understand all the rules so instead they play a glorified version of British Bulldog.

They drink like out of work actors, while court transcripts tend to show that their attitude towards sexual encounters could be described as a bit 'entitled'.

If they turn out to be any good they forget their principles and fuck off to warm the bench in union pretty sharpish.

Cricket

Wildly mercenary. When the whole world was united in horror and outrage at the racist regime in South Africa, it was the gentlemanly sport of cricket that showed the way by breaking the international boycott of the country in exchange for big piles of cash.

Professional cricketers pride themselves on playing for any country apart from the one that they were actually born in. Will kick over the stumps quicker than you can say "match fixing" if there are a few quid in it.

All they really want to do is fall into the stupid-haired, Instagram, roast-a-thon lifestyle that they have all craved since they weren't good enough to get into the football team at school.

THIS PAGE LEFT (PARTLY) INTENTIONALLY ALMOST ENTIRELY BLANK

Printed in Great Britain
by Amazon

52341611R00051